1,001 PROVERBS FROM TUNISIA

1,001 PROVERBS FROM TUNISIA

Isaac Yetiv

Preface by Hédi Bouraoui

An Original by Three Continents

Three Continents Press, Inc.
1636 Connecticut Ave., N.W.
Washington, D.C. 20009

Library of Congress Cataloging-in-Publication Data

Yetiv, Isaac, 1929–
1,001 proverbs from Tunisia

Each proverb is presented in transliterated Arabic, with a literal English translation, and alternative translations and/or explanatory material.
Includes index.

1. Proverbs, Arabic—Tunisia. 2. Proverbs, Arabic—Translations into English. 3. Proverbs, English—Translations from Arabic. I. Title. II. Title: One thousand one proverbs from Tunisia. III. Title: One thousand and one proverbs from Tunisia.

PN6519.A7Y48 1987 398'.9'92709611 87-10230
ISBN 0-89410-615-5
ISBN 0-89410-616-3 (pbk.)

Cover art by Max Winkler.

In memory of my father
YAACOV KIKI TIBI,
a fount of knowledge,
a rock of integrity.

Table of Contents

Preface/ix
Foreword/xi
Notes on the Transliteration/xiii

1,001 Proverbs from Tunisia/1

Thematic Index/151

Preface

A native Tunisian born in Nabeul in the Cap Bon, Isaac Yetiv has acquired since his childhood a mind full of proverbs, sayings, and aphorisms that he uses judiciously in every conversation one has with him.

A few years ago I was so impressed by his knowledge and command of Tunisian folklore, customs, and behaviors, and his perfect command of the language, that I pressed on him the need to save for posterity a treasure of wisdom belonging to Tunisia, or the old Ifrikia.

If Tunisia is well known for its historical past, Roman and Carthaginian, Byzantine, Turkish, Arab, and French, it is also so rich in its *imaginaire,* incessantly creating sayings and proverbs which form part of our heritage.

Therefore, Isaac Yetiv turned to the past to do research and add knowledge to his personal present time. He succeeded in gathering, symbolically, one thousand and one proverbs and sayings that he transcribed phonetically. He adopted a simple, accessible, and efficient transcription of the Tunisian proverbs. He did an excellent literal translation, which unfortunately does not always take into account the rhymes and rhythms of the dialectical Arabic. Indeed, all of the sayings recorded project a definite poetic dimension due to internal alliterations, rhythmic patternings, and parallel rhymings:

> mul ettaj yeẖtaj
>
> The crowned will [also] be in need.
>
> Even the king needs someone or something.

Isaac Yetiv gives us two versions of the proverb, but it is very difficult to seize the exact rhyming schemes of the original. In order to heighten the reader's comprehension, it seems necessary to de-emphasize the rhythmic schemes and patterns in order to concentrate on the signified, as opposed to the signifier. Isaac Yetiv provides alternatives to a literal translation and indeed he adds explanatory notes or gives a complete story setting the proverb in its proper historical and practical context. He has the talent for dramatizing these stories in a concise yet richly suggestive manner.

Needless to say, these proverbs can be extremely handy in every walk of life. They synthesize some of our complicated actions, shed light on our daily behavior, and indeed sum up powerfully and succinctly values which form part of humanity's ethics. The turn of mind of the proverbs, the way they are articulated, sometimes humorously, sometimes ironically, sometimes flippantly, sometimes mockingly, always demonstrates a vision of life which has a profound philosophical base.

What is interesting about these proverbs is that most of them do not present a didactic message. They are rather presented dramatically through a metaphoric patterning which leaves room for plural suggestions and interpretations, as in:

> ya mrabi ulad ennas yelli tsob elma felkeskas
>
> Raising other people's children is like pouring water in the colander.
>
> Against adoption.

Here the situation is so well-dramatized as to indicate that the efforts in raising one's child can be productive only if it is done by the involved, concerned parents. Otherwise, it is simply a waste of time. One can deduct from this a society turned inward on its family values, which can be both good and bad. The proverb leaves room for ambiguity and alternatives. It is not restricted to parenthood; it implies that any effort provided is bound to be more rewarding when one is totally committed.

As one can see from this example, each proverb can lead to so many interpretations, stretching our imagination and suggesting a lively, synthesized wisdom one can easily incorporate into one's own life.

Maghrebian studies have been flourishing in North America over the last twenty years. These proverbs will give us a richly textured background on the mores and behavior of this people. Professor Yetiv is to be commended for having gathered, transcribed, translated, and explained these Tunisian proverbs which form one of the most important components of world civilization. His book will be useful not only for ethnological, anthropological, and sociological research, but will also shed a great light on the literature produced by North Africa in Arabic, Berber, and French, since one encounters in the narrative structures of Maghrebian writers echoes or literal transformations of these proverbs. I am convinced that this collection is a landmark incorporating not only proverbs but sayings and *dictons.* I trust it will receive the wide attention it deserves. Perhaps even in the future it could be presented in the Arabic and French languages for a Maghrebian and world audience.

Hédi Bouraoui
York University
Toronto

Foreword

As a child growing up in Tunisia in a Jewish family, I was fascinated by the richness of the popular culture and folklore. I was among the lucky few who could observe and learn first-hand from the wise men, the carriers and transmitters of these treasures. I remember my father telling stories extolling the virtues of famous epic heroes to a charmed audience, or exchanging riddles with other wise men. But what left an indelible mark on me was the immense reservoir of proverbs and sayings into which he delved constantly, as he spoke, to embellish his tales, to captivate his audience, and to convince them of the veracity of the fantastic events and the powers of the supernatural. It was all poetry, rhymes and rhythms, clad in the garb of real events but wrapped in a cloak of mystic symbols and myths, a perfect synthesis of biblical and talmudic lore with the wonderful and supernatural world of the *Thousand and One Nights.* As an adolescent, I "graduated" from my father's "school" to devote myself to more "useful" activities such as my studies in the French High School and University. Many years later, I often found myself surrounded by attentive crowds, though much smaller than my father's, listening to my "proverbs." I became the legitimate heir and the transmitter of my generation. Sadly enough, with the awesome changes that mark our times, our children are not blessed with the same patience and thirst for knowledge of this treasure of oral literature. To protect it from oblivion and preserve it from extinction, I acceded to the wishes of my friends and colleagues at the African Literature Association to consign it to writing for posterity. Thus, I began the long process of gathering these proverbs by digging into my own memory, jotting down on tiny pieces of paper what popped into my mind at that moment. This provided me with a "capital" of about 250 proverbs, which encouraged me to pursue my endeavor. The balance of the symbolic number of 1,001 was gathered from lengthy interviews with members of the old generations, luckily still alive, dispersed over three continents.

This work is by no means exhaustive; it could certainly be improved and my gratitude is given in advance for any comments, suggestions, or corrections that the readers may offer. These proverbs are naturally the emanation of my own native milieu, the Jewish community of northeast Tunisia, but they are not exclusive to that area or ethnic group; with some changes, they are found all over the country and even in eastern Algeria.

The 1,001 proverbs are arranged alphabetically according to the English transliteration, which is followed by a literal translation, some annotations and explanations, and, when possible, the anecdote, story, or legend from which the proverb sprang. A thematic index of the most important subjects appears at the end of the book.

As for the transliteration, we have adopted a simplified system where each sound is represented by one single character. Its rules are explained in pages xiii-xiv.

I would like to express my thanks and gratitude to those who helped make this project a reality:

To my correspondents and interviewees who contributed the proverbs, through memory and research: my brothers Yossef Tibi and Shalom Tibi (Israel), my sisters Henrietta Tayeb (Israel) and Marie Tibi (Paris), my cousins Arki Tibi and Joseph Uzan (Israel), and all my friends: Daniel and Lydia Uzan (Israel), Albert Guez (Paris), Victor Haddad (Israel), Henri Guez Guejili (Tunis), David Koskas (Paris), Isaac Guez Bazaca and Lucie (Paris), Lalou Koskas (Paris), and Monique Hayoun (Paris).

To Professor Hédi Bouraoui (York University, Toronto), for his kind Preface and his steady encouragement, to my colleague Professor Claude Meade (University of Akron) for proofreading the English part of the manuscript, to our secretary Dorothy Richards and her assistant Rheadawn McGee for typing and retyping the manuscript.

My special thanks to Dr. Clairbourne E. Griffin, Dean of the College of Arts and Sciences, University of Akron, for his encouragement and assistance, without which this publication would not have been possible.

Isaac Yetiv
University of Akron
Akron, Ohio

Notes on the Transliteration

For the purpose of clarity and simplification, the following rules of transliteration will apply:

The Vowels. There are six vocalic sounds: a, e, è, i, o, u.

"a" is pronounced as in the English word "car"

"e" is pronounced as in the English word "met" (short)

"è" is pronounced as in the English word "bad" (long)

"i" is pronounced as in the English words "give" (short) or "seed" (long)

"o" is pronounced as in the English word "door"

"u" is pronounced as in the English words "put" (short) or "suit" (long)

The Consonants. Each Arabic consonantic sound is represented by a *single* English letter. Thus, the consonants b, d, f, g, h, k, l, m, n, s, t, w, y, and z are pronounced as in English.

"r" is rolled as in Spanish or Italian

the English "sh" sound is represented by "ś"

the English "th" sound, although extant in Arabic, has been omitted from this work and simply replaced by "t" or "d" to conform to the norms of the spoken language.

the consonant "j" is pronounced as in the French word "jour" or the English word "pleasure"

As for the five guttural Arabic sounds that have no equivalents in English:

ح is represented by "h̲" and pronounced as in "h̲ouse," but strongly aspired.

خ is represented by "x" and is pronounced as in the German word "mac̲h̲en"

ع is represented by the circumflex "ˆ" placed over the corresponding vowel: thus, we have â, ê, î, ô, and û. This sound is very difficult to pronounce for non-natives, who may approximate it by simply omitting the "ˆ" and pronouncing the vowel a, e, i, o, or u. When a vowel precedes this consonant, the symbol used is an apostrophe following the vowel: thus we have, for example, "a' " (for أع), and similarly e', i', o', and u'.

غ is represented by "ḡ" and pronounced as a velar French "r"

ق is represented by "q" and pronounced as a guttural "k" (again, not easy for non-natives).

1,001 PROVERBS FROM TUNISIA

Note: for each proverb, the transliterated Arabic is presented in **bold type.** *Literal translations appear in* roman type, *and alternative translation(s) and/or explanatory material appears in italic type.*

1. **âdiha âl h̲aluf iqolek mesta'jel**

Offer her to the pig, he will say "I am in a hurry."

Speaking of a woman—she is so ugly that even the pig will refuse her, using lack of time as an excuse.

2. **adrab elkelb uqadru fi wej mulah**

Hit the dog but honor him for the sake of his master.

You must suffer bad things because of fear or interest.

3. **adrab elqatusa txaf la'rusa**

Beat the cat, and the bride will be frightened.

If you want to be respected, or feared, show one example of your strength or courage, and everybody will understand that you mean business.

4. **adrbu belfula yetśaq**

Hit him with a bean, he will break.

He is very weak.

5. **âdu elkerś arbîn âm**

The enemy of the belly forty years.

If you deprive someone of food, he will be your enemy for forty years.

6. **ah̲an menni âla weldi kadab, wah̲ras menni âla mali xanab**

More compassionate than I toward my child is a liar, and more careful than I about my money is a cheater.

7. **aẖfad elmim taẖfdek**

Protect the M, it will protect you.

The M is the first letter of the negative "ma." Hence, if you say "no," you will be safe.

8. **aẖini elyom woqtelni ḡodwa**

Let me live today and kill me tomorrow.

Let's take things one by one, what is urgent first.

9. **aẖqarni urabi yetfakarni**

You despise me, but God will remember me.

Don't worry about men's attitudes toward you; the most important is God's.

10. **ahrab melqtar ja taẖt elmizèb**

He fled from the rain and came under the gutter.

Run from danger to danger, fall from the frying pan into the fire.

11. **âla âyn tetdara myèt âyn**

For one eye, one puts up with one hundred eyes.

If you like, fear, or respect one person, you must bear the burden of his companions, family, or friends.

12. **âla kerśu yexreb ôśu**

For his belly he will destroy his home.

13. **âlam yedeyk uxabihom iji elwaqt wiyatihom**

Teach your hands and hide them, time will come when they will be fit [for work].

Learn a trade, be prepared for the future, it will serve you.

14. **âla qad farśek otloq rojlek**

Stretch your leg to the size of your bed.

Know your limitations; do not think of yourself more than what you really are; do not live beyond your means.

15. **âla riẖet erriẖa habat êyneyh śriẖa**

    Just for smelling death, he cried his eyes out.

    He cried for the death of someone he does not even know; overzeal and false appearances.

16. **âla śahwtu yexreb naxwtu**

    For his desires, he destroys his reputation.

    He cannot resist the temptation to satisfy his sensual appetites, the pleasures of eating, drinking, sex, and because of that he ruins his health and reputation.

17. **âlaś xayef, âdabusa ula âla ras errajel?**

    What are you worring about? The bottle or the man's head?

    Human safety is more important than material losses.

18. **âlfu âm ma iâśikś leyla**

    Feed him for one year, he will not feed you for one night.

    This is said in response to a show of ingratitude from children, relatives, or friends for whom you have done big favors.

19. **âl qowt baû elyaqut, umelqowt lèmu elyaqut**

    For the food they sold pearls, and by saving on food they acquired pearls.

    You should eat moderately; too much expense can ruin you, too little may make you rich but will damage your health.

20. **ama merjal omok âyśa**

    What a man Mother Aisha is!

    This woman commands everyone, manages everything; she is the boss, stronger than all men surrounding her.

21. **a'mel ma a'mel jarek ula beddel darek**

Do what your neighbors did, or move out of your house.

You can't be different from your group, or neighbors, or peers; you will feel uncomfortable not "keeping up with the Joneses."

22. **a'mel nefsek mahbul tîs̀**

Pretend that you are crazy, you will live.

In some circumstances, it is better not to show your intelligence, in order not to arouse suspicion; play dumb, you will be safe.

23. **amman erriya fi fom elqatus!**

Trust the piece of lung in the mouth of the cat!

You will never get back a piece of meat from the mouth of a cat; if you lend something, or money, to a greedy and dishonest person, he will never return it.

24. **âm mśum yetâda, ray mśum ma yetâdaś**

A bad year will pass, a bad mind will not pass.

One will forget bad times and hardships, but will not bear a person with a negative mind, constant bad advice, and wrong attitudes.

25. **a'morha ma baxret, kif baxret ẖarqet ẖwayejha**

She has never burned incense; the first time she did, she burned her clothes.

Bad luck, or inexperience, can be harmful.

26. **ana bettamra lfomu uhuwa belûd lèyni**

I put a date in his mouth, and he puts a stick in my eye.

Ingratitude!

27. **ana ellẖam wenti essekkin**

I am the meat and you are the knife.

I am now in your hands, your captive, or your dependent; I will do what you say, and will follow you without questions.

28. **ana ğniya wenẖab lehdiya**

I am wealthy and I still like to receive gifts.

There is more in a gift than its material value.

29. **ana ma somtś sidi kabur nsum estir elgaẖba!**

I did not fast on the Holy Yom Kippur [Jewish day of atonement], and you want me to fast for the whore Esther?

In the pre-Islamic era in North Africa, there was a strong movement of conversion to Judaism among the native population of the Berbers. One day, a Jew explained to one of these "converts" the meaning of a fast in memory of the Queen Esther who saved her people by accepting marriage the Persian King Ahasverus. The Berber reacted as said.

In the figurative, this proverb is used in an a fortiori *argument such as: "I don't even smoke cigarettes, you want me to smoke marijuana?" or "I avoid him at the club, you want me to invite him to dinner?"*

30. **ana nâyet wessorraq tenzad**

I yell, and there are more thieves.

Complaining makes it worse.

31. **ana nesni wejjabya maqûra**

I keep filling, but the basin has a hole in it.

Useless work, or, one talks and nobody listens.

32. **ana wejmel sweyna myèt ryal**

I and the camel are worth 100 *ryal* [unit of currency].

A farmer brought to the market, for sale, a camel and a rooster. The rooster said that he and the camel together cost 100 ryal. *Of course, the price of a rooster is insignificant compared to that of a camel.*

This proverb is used against those who think much of them-

selves undeservedly and keep comparing themselves to the mighty and the famous.

33. **ana wenti umen sraq elfès?**

You and I and who stole the pick?

The situation is clear: either you *did it or* I *did it, because nobody else was here.*

34. **ând a'wah tesma' zwah**

When he goes to the bathroom to relieve himself, you will hear his screams.

The story is about someone who ate so much cactus fruit that he became constipated. In the figurative: the day of reckoning will come for those big spenders who cry when the bill is due. One must not overindulge in anything.

35. **ândi kmara ândkom ama kol śey marhun**

I own much property but everything is mortgaged.

Rich but living in poverty; he has possessions but cannot, or would not, enjoy them.

36. **âned elqfel uma tâned elfqar**

You may overcome a miser but not a poor man.

Give your daughter to a rich man even if he is a miser (because there will always be something for her) and not to a poor man (who has nothing to give).

37. **a'qab elmèl mèl wa'qab ezzeyn zeyn**

What remains of wealth is still wealth, and what remains of beauty is still beauty.

Even old, a beautiful woman is still beautiful.

38. **âql ennsa zeynhom uzeyn errjal âqlhom**

A woman's intelligence is her beauty and a man's beauty is his intelligence.

The best quality for a woman is her beauty, and for a man it's his intelligence.

39. **arbat bhimek ma' leẖmir, ida ma yetâlam eśśhiq yetâlam ennhiq**

Tie your young donkey with the old ones; if he does not learn to yell, he will learn to bray.

When you live with someone, you learn his habits.

40. **armih men estaẖ iji waqef**

Throw him from the roof, he falls standing on his feet.

He is very lucky.

41. **armi ruẖek felbir uqul elmlayka dezzetni**

Throw yourself in the well and say the angels pushed me.

Don't blame others for your own acts; be responsible.

42. **aś ândi felgamẖ ida ḡla, rajel oma ikeyla**

Why do I have to worry about the increase in the price of wheat; my stepfather will pay for it.

One worries about expenses only when one pays for them; or, those who do not go to war don't worry about its dangers.

43. **âś bujbeyba ubujbeybteyn ubublaś**

Everybody lives, the one who has one coat, the one who has two, and even the one who has none.

One can survive with less.

44. **âsfur felyed ula myè itiru**

A bird in the hand is better than 100 flying.

A bird in the hand is worth two in the bush. Little and sure is better than much in the air.

45. **âsfur xla matmur**

A bird destroyed a cave.

Even a small and weak person (or animal) can be very destructive.

46. **aslek aslek ya soltan**

Even kings behave according to their upbringing.

Nature is stronger than nurture, even in high social positions.

47. **aś qolt ya tbib ana ndawi welmard izid**

Doctor, what did you say? I cure, and the disease gets worse.

One tries to remedy a situation, and he makes it worse. Sometimes, lack of action is better than action.

48. **âtalnakom, alla la yarẖmelna waldeyn**

We disturbed you, may God curse us.

When you do a favor for someone or try to help, and he does not appreciate it, you use this proverb sarcastically.

49. **âteytu faẖ, kleytu raẖ**

I gave it, the word spread about it; I ate it, it was lost.

Giving food to the poor is better than consuming it unnecessarily; it also enhances one's reputation.

50. **âtini qartalti umaẖajtiś be'neb**

Give me my basket, I don't need the grapes.

A told B to bring him a basket which A will fill with grapes for B. When B returned for his basket and the grapes, A told him to come back the next day. This was repeated for many days. Then, out of impatience, B asked for his basket without *the grapes.*

Just give me my things, don't do me any favor.

51. **âwen ennsara ula qa'dek xsara**

Help [even] the Christians [people of other religions]; doing nothing is a waste of time.

Don't sit idle; do something, even if it is profitable only to strangers.

52. **axsar ufaraq uqul mella raẖa**

Lose, and separate yourself, and say "good riddance!"

If you join a partnership, or make any deal, or get married, and discover later that it is undesirable, or that you are losing much money, it is better to quit rather than continue to suffer pain or losses.

53. **âyn latra qalb layuja'**

The eye will not see, and the heart will not ache.

If you don't see a bad thing, you won't suffer.

54. **âyn leẖsud fiha ûd**

A log in the eye of the envious.

This is said sometimes to ward off the evil eye. It is also a warning not to be jealous or to covet what other people have.

55. **âynu assaẖ melfès**

His eye is stronger than a pick.

He lies in your face, and when you confront him, he continues to lie unashamedly.

56. **âyta weśhud âla dbiẖet qanfud**

Yelling and witnesses for the slaughtering of a hedgehog.

Much ado about nothing.

57. **âzeb bekâlu ula śayeb bmalu**

A young bachelor with his filth is better than an old man with his wealth.

It is better for a girl to marry a poor young man than a rich old man.

58. **âzuza uśadet saraq**

An old woman who caught a thief.

Seizing an opportunity and taking advantage of it; the old woman who catches the thief that has been stealing from her for a long time will punish him severely.

59. **baâd tjib leẖtab**

Go far away, you will bring wood.

Don't be promiscuous, keep your distances, you will be respected.

60. **ba'bus elkelb arbîn âm fettext yoxroj mâwej**

A dog's tail, even after 40 years of stretching, will come out crooked.

Nature is stronger than nurture.

61. **ba'd arbîn âm ya rajel âynek âwra?**

After 40 years: hey man, you are one-eyed!

After having lived with a husband for a long time, it is awkward and fake to find fault with him. Also applies to other situations.

62. **ba'd la'dam ma yenfa' enndam**

After harm is done, regret is worthless.

63. **ba'd lakẖal ma yosbog̅ sabag̅**

After black, no dyeing [color] is possible.

There is nothing we can do; the problem has no solution; or, he will never regain honor and respect; he is beyond repair.

64. **ba'd ma baset lemmet fxadha**

After she farted, she tightened her legs.

An attempt to redress a wrong after it is done is worthless.

65. **ba'd ma èxèd śra mkohla**

After he was robbed, he bought a gun.

After damage is done, one can do nothing. One must be prepared to prevent, not to act after fact.

66. **ba'd ma śab mśa lelkutab**

After he became old, he went to school.

Education starts at a young age; it is worthless for old people.

67. **ba'd ma talaqha âwed âśaqha**

After he divorced her, he returned to love her.

After a matter is closed, one reopens Pandora's box.

68. **ba'd ma tzawjet kotru elxataba**

After she got married, many men asked for her hand.

When we need something, we don't have it; when we don't need it, it comes in abundance.

69. **ba'd omi ma nhaman hajala**

After [I saw what] my mother [did], I will never trust a widow.

A woman needs the company of a man; a widow cannot be trusted.

70. **ba'd rkubek âl masriya rkebt âla bhèyem nakas**

After you rode the famous mare, you rode a skittish donkey.

After your past wealth and splendor, you are reduced to this! (having fallen from the social ladder).

71. **baqi lehbel âjjarara**

The rope is always on the pulley.

Life goes on; things continue to happen; nothing changes.

72. **baqi wezman ilaqi**

Bear [the hardship], time will help heal.

73. **bar leẖrir ẖata mesẖu bih etnajer!**

Has silk become so cheap that it is used to mop pots!

This proverb is used when a person who is wealthy, respected, a member of high society, is ruined and everybody then despises him.

74. **bat âla ḡoś umatbatś âla ndama**

Go to sleep over anger, and don't go to sleep over regret.

It is better to stay angry with someone than to commit a violent act which you will regret later.

75. **bat bla âśa wesbaẖ bla deyn**

Go to bed hungry and wake up without debt.

Do not use other people's money for your own needs; restrict your spending, and don't borrow even for necessities.

76. **beflusi ma nosẖob jazar**

With my money, I don't need to befriend the butcher.

I want no favors; I pay for everything.

77. **beflusi nakol elẖalwa**

With my money, I will eat candies.

I can do anything I want with my money; nobody can prevent me from spending as much as I want.

78. **belli ibi' essareq rabaẖ**

Whatever the price a thief will get, he is a winner.

When you don't invest anything, you don't worry. Easy come, easy go.

79. **bent eśśarq lelḡarb ubent elḡarb leśśarq**

The Oriental girl will go the the Occident [West]; and the

Western girl to the Orient.

God's ways are mysterious; nobody knows his own destiny.

80. **berzana taba' uśuf**

With patience, follow and look!

Don't rush; don't jump to conclusions.

81. **bettalq katar ennafqa**

On credit, buy more.

When you buy on credit, you spend more money because you feel you don't have to pay now. This is a warning against borrowing.

82. **beyn elloqma welfom tama ẖakem yoẖkom**

Between the spoonful and the mouth, there is a ruler that rules.

God can save the righteous (or punish the wicked) in the twinkle of an eye.

83. **beyt bla korsi qul ledayf emśi**

A house without a chair, tell the guest to leave.

If you want to entertain guests, you must be equipped for it, or don't invite anyone to your house.

84. **bhim eśśerka imut modbar**

The donkey who has two masters will die full of sores.

Partnership is bad.

85. **bhim gdem qarà**

A donkey bit a pumpkin.

No big deal, it happens every day.

86. **bi' weśri uśarek ennas fi mwalha**

Sell and buy and take a share of the wealth.

Commerce makes you rich.

87. **bkotrot elham idaẖak**

Too much trouble and sorrow makes you laugh.

Sometimes, when you are overwhelmed by problems, the best answer is laughter.

88. **bkotrot errias yoḡroq elmerkeb**

Many captains sink the ship.

Only one person should be in command, make decisions, and bear responsibility.

89. **bkotrot essnaya' tla' daya'**

Because he has so many trades, he is unemployed.

This is said about a person who knows a little of everything, and can do nothing well.

90. **bla' essekkina bdamha**

He swallowed the knife with its blood.

He did not leave any trace of his crime, or of any other bad action.

91. **blaśi blaśi mesûd yebki kamal raẖlu bhimu**

He is used to crying for no reason; now that he has lost his donkey, you can imagine how much he will cry.

The situation is already very bad, and what has just happened makes it even worse.

92. **bna uâla mśa uxala**

He built, higher and higher; he departed and left everything after him.

In your life, you build and accumulate wealth, but you will die and leave everything after you. No use amassing wealth; better enjoy yourself while still alive; life is short.

93. **bu iqum bâśra uâśra ma iqumuś bbuhem**

A father can support ten [children]; ten cannot support their father.

94. **buk ih̲abek ḡnia urajlek ih̲abek qwiya**

Your father wants you to be rich and your husband wants you to be strong.

Everyone wishes things to be in his own interest.

95. **bul felxreb qbel ma iwelliw jwama'**

Urinate in the wrecked slums before they become mosques.

Hit now before your enemy grows stronger. Seize the opportunity.

96. **buôryan usabu âlih elmelh̲**

A slug, and they poured salt on it.

A situation is already bad and you aggravate it. The slug is slimy and disgusting, but at least alive; by putting salt on it, you destroy it completely.

97. **bus elkelb fi fomu h̲ata teqdi h̲ajtek menu**

Kiss the dog on his mouth until you take what you need from him.

When you need someone, you kiss him and pretend to love him until you get what you want from him.

98. **bus yed essana' uma tbus yed elârf**

Kiss the hand of the apprentice and don't kiss the hand of the boss.

Sometimes the subordinate wields more power than the master, and will help more eagerly.

99. **da' lebhim beyn Mixayel u Gebriyel**

The donkey is lost between Michael and Gabriel.

Two people fight and a third is the victim.

100. **darba belmtarqa udarba belmemlsa**

One blow with the hammer and one with the trowel.

A time to hit and a time to soothe. Applies to education.

101. **darba fi ḡeyr jenbi kif elli fi h̲ayt**

A blow on the ribs of somebody else is like a blow on the wall.

Nobody feels the real pain of others; you only feel pain in your own flesh.

102. **darba men yed mâlam ula myè men yed sana'**

One creative act from an accomplished artist is better than one hundred from an apprentice.

If you need some work or advice, always go to the experts.

103. **darb elhajala fi bentha**

It is like the widow hitting her daughter.

She does it very softly and with pity for the orphan.

104. **dar berjal ula dar belmal**

A house full of men is better than a house full of money.

105. **dar bla kbir kif sènyè bla bir**

A house without an elderly master is like a field without a well.

Age and experience are very important.

106. **dar bla sḡar kif jneyna bla nawar**

A house without children is like a garden without flowers.

107. **darb lemnah̲ teffah̲**

A beating from good people is like apples.

Punishment is sometimes a good means of education.

108. **dar ennajar bla mḡorfa**

The house of the carpenter is without a spoon.

In old times, spoons were made of wood, and it is surprising that a carpenter would not have spoons, or that a shoemaker would go barefoot.

109. **dar essyuda ma ixośuha eddyab**

In the house of the lions, the wolves do not enter.

Only the weak are attacked; the strong are feared.

110. **dari dari ya sataret âri**

My house is a good cover for my misfortune, poverty, or scandal.

When you close your house, nobody sees, or hears, your problems, disease, or quarrels.

111. **dar lexla tbi' elleft**

The house of the desert sells turnips.

In a period of scarcity, even tasteless vegetables such as turnips can be sold.

112. **dayf leyla âdilu ahbalu**

Your one-night guest, accept his craziness.

Any passing difficulty (not eternal) can be easily endured.

113. **dayf leyla ma twarih faqrek**

Do not show your poverty to a one-night guest.

There is no need to volunteer information about your financial difficulties to strangers and passers-by.

114. **dbaret elfar âla mul eddar: bi' elqatusa weśri jebna**

The advice of the mouse to the owner of the house: sell the cat and buy cheese.

If someone gives you advice, it is in his own interest.

115. **dellel ya dallal uḇaraj welli ma yeśri yetfaraj**

Auction off, auctioneer, and let the non-buyers watch the show.

Applies when a person or a family is the object of a scandal that has become public.

116. **dexltu melâtba tjib elhem lerrekba**

His entering, from the threshold, brings worry [and fear] to the knees.

He is "bad news"; don't let him approach you.

117. **dexlu eldarek ixaraj ârek**

Let him in your house, he will take out your bad secrets.

Be careful in the choice of your guests, especially when you have "skeletons in the closet."

118. **dexlu yetlawa xarju yetqawa**

When he comes in, he is weak and submissive; when you want him out, he becomes strong and arrogant.

An act of compassion may result in much distress to the do-gooder.

119. **dièfet ennabi tlat ayam**

Hospitality, even for the prophet, is no more than three days.

A prolonged stay of a guest may sour the relationship.

120. **dièfet ennhar ziara**

Hospitality for one day is a visit.

If a guest stays only one day, one must do everything to please him, because it is short and bearable.

121. **drabha uẖaram âliha elbka**

He beat her and forbade her to cry.

To add insult to injury, to compound one's cruelty by doing harm to someone and preventing him from complaining or crying.

122. **drab ubka umśa lelqadi śka**

He hit [him], he cried, and he went to complain to the judge.

Not all plaintiffs are right; they may be at fault, but pretend to have been wronged to cover their crime.

123. **draêk ya âlaf**

Your arm [strength], you, good eater.

If you find something to eat, eat as much as you can. Take advantage of an opportunity while it lasts.

124. **dxal eldèxel ulbès lexlaxel**

He penetrated inside and wore the jewels [foot bracelets].

After he was allowed in, he took possession of the property and acted as master while he was only a guest.

125. **ebât weldek lessuq ijiblek metlu**

Send your son to market, he will bring you friends of his kind.

Birds of a feather flock together.

126. **eddar dar buna wennas itarduna**

The house is our father's and they have thrown us out.

Not only did they steal our property, but they also evicted us from it. Double victimization.

127. **eddar dar ejjabana wessaken raẖel**

The real dwelling place is the cemetery; the dwellers of the earth are only passengers [to the cemetery].

Life is short; we will all die.

128. **eddayf dayf walu ikun śta mâ sayf**

A guest is a guest even if he stays winter and summer.

Anything temporary is bearable.

129. **eddayf ebjel men buk**

Your guest takes precedence over your father.

130. **eddebana ma toqtolś ama tdara' elxlayeq**

The fly does not kill, but is very bothersome.

131. **eddeban ya'ref âla wej śkun yexra**

The flies know on whose face to shit.

If you are attacked, it is because you are weak; if a woman is accosted by a man, it is because she is loose.

Respect yourself and you will be respected by others.

132. **eddek fejjifa h̲ram**

Stabbing a corpse is forbidden.

After somebody dies, don't say evil things about him. Don't flog a dead horse.

133. **eddenya mâ elwaqef**

The world is with the strong of the moment.

One must submit to the powers that be.

134. **eddib kif ma lh̲aqś eddalia qal elânqud mor**

The wolf that could not reach the grapes said they are bitter.

Finding excuses for one's failures; sour grapes.

135. **eddrahem darhmumi wella esmi yendkar, kont weld gah̲ba welleyt si Elh̲aj Ali Bakar**

When I became rich, my name was on all lips; I was a "son of a bitch" and I became "Sir Haj Ali Bakar."

When he was poor, nobody believed him when he said that the mouse had eaten the cheese; when he became rich, everybody believed his story that the mouse had eaten the hammer. Money brings respect and credibility.

136. **edwam yenqob errxam**

Persistence and perseverance can make a hole even in marble.

You can do almost anything if you are patient and per-

severant. Do not despair after a few failures, try again.

137. **eftah̲ babek wetfaxar ula sakar babek westatar**

Open your door and show off, or close your door and hide.

If you have nothing to show for, don't boast and brag; know your limitations.

138. **ejbal ma tetlaqa ama erjal tetlaqa**

Mountains will not meet, but men will meet.

You may have succeeded this time in cheating me, but we will meet again and I will take my revenge.

139. **ejbed ma trod ejbal tethėd**

Draw and don't put back, [even] the mountains will be destroyed.

Spending all the time without having income will lead to ruin.

140. **ejjo' elli ibekki sḡarek ilezzek ala kol duni**

The hunger that makes your children cry will force you into all bad acts.

141. **ejmaȃ teḡleb essoltan**

The multitude is stronger than the king.

There is strength in numbers.

142. **ejmel ihez welqardana teqhar**

The camel bears the burden and the flea [the parasite on the camel] complains.

I do the work and you complain of fatigue; I lose the money and you cry over it!

143. **ejmel ma iśufś h̲adbtu**

The camel does not see its hump.

One does not see one's own defects.

144. **ejnaza ẖamya welmiyet kelb**

There is a lot of commotion at the funeral, and the deceased is [only] a dog.

Much ado about nothing.

145. **ekteb âjran useyeb felma**

Write on the frogs and throw in the water.

Do something useless; no trace will remain of it.

146. **elâdad uqallet elqabd**

Numbers without value.

Quantity but no quality.

147. **elâjala men eśśitan**

Speed is from the devil.

Don't rush, take your time, weigh the pros and cons.

148. **elâjuza ma ihemha elqars**

The old woman is not afraid of pinching [because pinching is not likely to lead to a more intimate relationship].

You can do nothing to me, you have no power over me; I am not afraid of you.

149. **elâlama felkbir kif edabra felbhim**

Teaching an old man is like an open sore on a donkey [it never heals].

What you are doing is useless.

150. **ela'ma iẖab melqfa a'yun**

The blind would like to have eyes even on the backs of their heads.

Anything is better than nothing; half a loaf is better than no loaf.

151. **elâm kolu ḫafi ja nhar egeyn lbès sabat**

The whole year he walks barefoot, but on the day of *egeyn* ["to lament" in Berber; a Jewish mourning day commemorating the destruction of the Temple. The tradition is to wear bad shoes or none], he wore nice shoes.

He does everything at counter-purpose; he does not follow logic, tradition, or common sense; he irritates others by his behavior.

152. **elâmŝa fi dar lo'mi kaḫlet elûyun**

A weak-eyed woman in the house of the blind is a blue-eyed woman.

Blues eyes, because of their scarcity in Tunisia, are a symbol of beauty. The relativity of our interpretations.

153. **elaqareb âqareb**

Relatives are scorpions.

Most hatred and jealousy is found in the family.

154. **elârd kif elbellar, ida tkasar ma yetjabar**

Honor is like glass; once broken, it cannot be put back together.

155. **ela'war beyn ello'mi soltan**

The one-eyed person among the blind is a king.

All is relative: beauty, intelligence, wealth, strength, are not absolute, but must be compared with others'.

156. **elâyn felqatuna welyed felma'juna**

The eye is on the girl and the hand is in the jam.

He is not really interested in the obvious thing; his interest is in something else.

157. **elâyn bsira welyed qsira**

The eye sees and the hand is short.

You see danger, evil acts, or crimes, and you can do nothing to help.

158. **el âzeb qandil, elmzewej mendil, elmtalaq dalil**

The bachelor is a candle, the married man a towel, and the divorced man miserable.

Maybe it would have been better if you never married, but now that you have, stay married because divorcing is even worse.

159. **elbelġa welmra ma fihom śerka**

The shoes and the wife cannot afford partners.

The stress is, of course, on the second part.

160. **elbent ulatha śmata wa'qabha ẖsada**

The daughter brings joy to our enemies in the beginning, and envy in the end.

You may be unhappy when a daughter is born (instead of a son), but in your old days, you can count on her much more.

161. **elbey sma' welqadi tba'**

The king has heard and the religious leader has put his seal.

The thing is done, finished, over with; there is no appeal.

162. **elbey yetenâl fi ḡyèbu; kif yaẖdar yetbèsu rkèybu**

[Even] the king can be cursed in his absence; when he returns, they kiss his knees.

One is only bound by the social duty of being polite and considerate in the face of others, but his freedom of speech is total behind their backs.

163. **elbir elli tośrob menu, ma tarmi fih ẖajra**

Do not throw a stone in a well from which you drink water.

Do not bite the hand that feeds you.

164. **elbnadem bḡamza welbhim bhamza**

Man needs only a hint, but the donkey needs pushing.

165. **elèhdiya ltunes welxra âla Sleyman**

The gift is for Tunis, and the excrement for Sleyman.

The city of Sleyman in Tunisia is on the way to Tunis, the capital. Travelers make a stop there just to relieve themselves. Applies when one gets all the credit and another gets the blame; or one pays the expenses and the other gets all the pleasure.

166. **elfartasa tetfaxar beśâr oxtha**

The bald woman boasts of her sister's hair.

Do not brag about other people's accomplishments or qualities; you deserve praise only for your own.

167. **elfarx izaqaq buh?**

Does the chick feed his father?

Don't teach me! I know better than you; I am older than you.

168. **elfès fidek welǵaba twalik**

The ax is in your hand, and the forest is at your disposal.

You have "carte blanche," full power to do what you want.

169. **elflus taẖi ennfus wettaher elmenjus wetrod eśśayeb ârus**

Money gives life, purifies the unclean, and makes the old man a newlywed.

The power of money is unlimited.

170. **elfom essaket ma teḋxolu debana**

In a silent mouth, the fly will not enter.

If you don't say anything you will not get in trouble.

171. **elfoxra leddud wetrab**

The praise goes only to worms and dust.

Worms and dust are eternal and destroy the corpses of the dead, while man is mortal.

172. **elf xatwa ula tengiza**

One thousand steps are better than one jump.

Don't rush into anything; be patient.

173. **elgods lekbir ixallaf qarfa**

A big pile will leave some scraps.

When a rich person becomes poor, there is always something left of his past riches.

174. **elḡula âmlet ôrs klatu hiya wuladha**

The ogress prepared a wedding feast, and she and her children ate everything.

True, you worked very hard, but it was for your sole benefit.

175. **elẖadeq bḡamza welbhim bhamza**

An intelligent person needs only a hint to understand what you say, but a dumb one needs shaking.

176. **elẖajra ma tdub, welqaẖba ma ttub**

The stone will never melt, and the whore will never repent.

The stress is on the second half: it is very difficult, even impossible, to abandon bad habits and change for good.

177. **elẖayt qsir ya belgasem**

The wall is short, Belgasem [everybody can climb over it].

He is a sucker; everybody takes advantage of him.

178. **elhendi mlih̲ walu bśewku**

The cactus fruit is given free; take it even if it has thorns.

Don't look a gift horse in the mouth.

179. **elh̲enna h̲arśa welh̲anana âmśa welârusa tarśa**

The henna is rough, the cosmetologist is blind, and the bride is deaf.

It is the tradition to have the bride's hair, hands, and feet covered with henna—here, the three important factors (henna, cosmetologist, and bride) have problems. What kind of a wedding will it be? Nothing works!

180. **elh̲enna ma tfut welâtar ma imut**

The wedding will not be over, and the grocer will not die.

There is no need to rush.

181. **elh̲ma h̲oma, esselfa âqrab sama, welkenna aâr melli tama**

The mother-in-law is a problem, the sister-in-law is a scorpion, and the daughter-in-law is worse than anything.

182. **elh̲sab itawel elôśra**

The account lengthens the friendship.

Short reckonings make long friends.

183. **elkbira bsa' wesḡira bsa'?**

The big one for a measure and the small one for the same measure?

All things don't have the same value; people are different; situations are different.

184. **elkelb mat uxalaf jarw tla' enten men abih**

The dog died and left a puppy that was worse than his father.

From bad, comes worse; it is better to resign yourself to a bad situation than change it and fall into a worse one.

185. **elkelb ma yahrob mel kesra**

The dog will not flee from a piece of bread.

No one will refuse to take something given to him.

186. **elkessèba tekseb wettaẖana teẖseb**

The rich will possess and the cuckolds will count.

It is better to work hard and make money than do nothing but count what other people make, and be jealous of them.

187. **elklam foda weskat dhab**

Words are silver, silence is gold.

188. **elklam maâ elli mayefhmekś xsara ula naqs fello'mor**

Talking to someone who does not understand you is a waste, or even worse, a shortening of your life.

189. **elklam mâk wellowm âla jartek**

The words are for you but the reproach is for your neighbor.

This applies when you attack someone (usually the weak) but you intend your words, or acts, against the more powerful whom you prefer not to confront.

190. **elkluf tẖabelhem ras elmal**

If you want to interfere in any matter, you need capital.

Put your money where your mouth is.

191. **elkobr ma iâliś lelmanbar**

Pride will not bring you to the podium.

You can achieve success not by being proud but by work and humility.

192. **ellaẖya elli tbusha beryal natafha beryaleyn**

The beard which you kiss for one *ryal*, pull it for two.

Sometimes, to save your honor and dignity, you tell someone off rather than kiss him, even if it costs you heavily.

193. **ellaẖya saba ama la'qal âjruda**

The beard is full but the brain is empty [like straw without grain].

He is old and should normally be wise, but he is dumb.

194. **ellexer mrawha qatêtha elxadem**

The last fan was broken by the servant.

Servants, usually, are very careful not to break things. In this case, a servant broke the last fan left for the comfort of her master who apparently has broken all the others. In the figurative, this proverb means: after so many losses, when something of value was left and we could count on it, it was destroyed by the person least expected to do it. In one word: no luck!

195. **elleyl budeynatu wenhar ba'weynatu**

Night has its ears; day has its eyes.

Be careful and discreet day and night, because even if you may not be seen at night, you may be heard. Keep your secrets to yourself.

196. **ellẖam ida yenten ma ilu kan emalih**

When the meat is rotten, its owner must eat it or dispose of it.

If a person strays from the right way, or is the victim of fate, the family must take care of him, not strangers.

197. **elli âmlu fi soḡru zanu, elli âmlu fi kobru śanu**

Doing it when you are young is nice; doing it when you are old is ugly.

Everything in its time is good.

198. **elli ându lekâb yelâb**

He who has the chips [as in a casino] may play [or gamble].

It is OK to spend much money if you have it, and, of course, it is bad to live beyond your means by borrowing and spend-

ing money that you don't have.

199. **elli ându maqrud felmezwed la ijih ennowm ula yorqod**

One who has pastry in the cupboard will not be able to sleep.

He worries about being robbed. The poor have nothing to worry about.

200. **elli ându śweya zeft iqalab elmrakeb weyn trasi**

He has a little tar, and he is looking for the docks [so that he can fix the damaged boats].

He has delusions of grandeur.

201. **elli âta bentu ѐyes rgadha**

After giving your daughter in marriage, you are no longer responsible for her honor, how or with whom she sleeps. It becomes her husband's responsibility.

202. **elli âta fi ẖyatu tlab allah umag̃atu**

He who gives [his wealth] during his life, will ask God's help and will not get it.

203. **elli âta kelmtu âta raqbtu**

He who gave his word gave his neck.

One must keep one's promise.

204. **elli ba' mѐzѐl ibi'**

He who sold is still selling.

If you rejoice at my misfortune, you may one day be in the same situation, because God who did that to me may do it to you too.

205. **elli beddel lbasu ma beddel rasu**

By changing your clothing you do not change your head.

The clothing is only superficial, for the sake of appearance; what counts is your head and what is in it.

206. **elli bih sekra bih sabat**

Instead of using the money for alcohol, better buy shoes.

207. **elli bowsa tradih la xeyr fih**

He who can be reconciled with a kiss is not worth much.

If someone has been wronged, it is not enough to kiss him or to apologize. He needs more: repentance, making amends, and promises not to do it again.

208. **elli fenâma ma yośkor, yoxroj menha uma yośôr**

He who is not thankful in prosperity will leave it without noticing it.

Count your blessings and thank God for what you have while you have it.

209. **elli fèt mèt**

What is past is dead.

What is done is done; don't cry over spilled milk.

210. **elli fidu kol yom îdu**

When one has money, every day is a holiday for him.

If you have the means, you can spend your money in pleasures and feasts. No one can blame you for it.

211. **elli flusu fi jibu ma iban êybu**

He who has money in his pocket, nobody sees his defects.

One overlooks the defects of the rich; their wealth hides their defects, and their misconduct is tolerated.

212. **elli ḡab ḡab sehmu**

If one is absent, his share is absent.

The absent are always losers.

213. **elli ẖaj ẖaj welli âwaq âwaq**

Some succeed in reaching Mecca for the pilgrimage and some die on the way.

Everything is a matter of luck; one must accept one's fate.

214. **elli iâdi bh̲ar iâdi bh̲ayra**

He who passes a sea will pass a little lake.

We have seen worse in our lives; we will overcome this, too.

215. **elli iâdi kelma iâdi jbel**

He who passes a word passes a mountain.

A hard word or an insult, overlooked, is a courageous deed.

216. **elli ibeddel lah̲ya blah̲ya yeśtaqhem etneyn**

He who substitutes a beard for another beard will lose both.

When you change jobs, or places, you don't enjoy any of them. Be content with what you have.

217. **elli ibèt leyla ma' edjaj yesbah̲ iqaqi**

He who spends a night with a chicken will cackle in the morning.

You learn the habits of those with whom you live.

218. **elli ibiêk belful biû belqśur**

If someone sells you for a handful of fava beans, sell him for the skins of the beans.

If somebody does not respect you, you should respect him even less.

219. **elli ih̲abek ibèkik welli yekrhek yedh̲ak âlik**

Those who love you will make you cry, and those who hate you will laugh at you.

Don't take nice words from your enemy; the truth comes out only from friends, however bitter it may be.

220. **elli ih̲abek isaqatlek welli yekrhek ilaqatlek**

Those who love you will overlook your faults and those who hate you will nitpick on you.

221. **elli ih̲ab elkol yeddi elkol**

He who wants all loses all.

Don't be greedy; be content with little.

222. **elli ih̲ab ellellu yeshar elleyl bkellu**

If you enjoy the pleasures, then you have to stay awake for the whole night.

You have nothing for nothing; there is no such thing as a free lunch.

223. **elli ih̲ab ezzeyn ma yesteğlaś elmahr**

If you like beauty, you should not discuss the amount of the dowry.

The groom pays a dowry to the bride's father. A beautiful bride commands a higher dowry.

If you want quality, you pay for it.

224. **elli ih̲abha men jneynetha ih̲abha men metbexha**

If you love her [when she comes] from the garden, you must also love her [when she comes] from the kitchen.

One must accept the bad with the good in life.

225. **elli ih̲ab ifarah̲ nefsu yetfakar leylet ồrsu**

He who would like to be happy will remember his wedding night.

226. **elli ih̲ab iqalal ahnah isekken nsibu bah̲dah**

He who wants to disturb his tranquility will bring his son-in-law to live with him.

227. **elli ih̲ab isèmûlek yeh̲kiwlek h̲tit**

If he wants you to hear something, he will tell you the story on behalf of someone else.

People who tell you something as said by others express their own opinion indirectly.

228. **elli ih̲ab iśuf eddenia ba'du iśufha ba'd ḡeyru**

If you want to see the world you leave after you, see it after the others.

When someone dies, nothing will change after him; only the deceased loses his life.

229. **elli ih̲abu rabi izèyenlu xliqtu ula ixafaflu mleyktu**

When God loves someone, He will give him a beautiful face or a pleasant personality.

230. **elli ih̲ab yerkeb âjmel yeh̲mel basu**

If you like to ride a camel, you must endure his farts.

No roses without thorns.

231. **elli imut yetwalu saqeyh**

When somebody dies, his legs become longer.

After death, people usually praise the deceased even if he does not deserve it.

232. **elli iqadar iqadar nefsu**

He who honors honors himself.

Honor and respect are mutual. When you respect someone, he will respect you.

233. **elli iqalal qowtu âjal âla mowtu**

If you reduce your food intake, you hasten your death.

Save on anything else, but not on food.

234. **elli iqul elh̲aq rasu yetśaq**

If you tell the truth, your head will be cracked.

By telling the truth, you will get into trouble; people don't like to hear the truth about themselves.

235. **elli isèwèd weju iwelli fah̲am**

By painting his face black, he became a coal dealer.

It is not the appearance that makes you a real expert, but knowledge, experience, and hard work.

236. **elli ixalaf men umur eśar' yehtajelhom**

If you do not observe all the laws [of religion, society, justice], you will need them.

Another time, you will be the victim of the same behavior by others.

237. **elli ixalet ixalet kèn men dar kbira; ida ma yetâśa ibèt fedfa**

Choose your company [and friends, or wife] from among the rich and powerful; that way, even if you don't dine, you will at least find a warm bed.

238. **elli ixalet qowm yerja' mennu**

If you socialize with certain people, you become like them.

239. **elli ixallat la'sel yelh̲as swabû**

One whose job is to mix the honey will lick his fingers [and eat honey in the process].

Those who are close to the pie will have part of it.

240. **elli ixelli âśah leḡdah ma yeśmtuś fih âdah**

He who leaves his dinner for the next day will not give his enemies the satisfaction of seeing him in poverty.

Never show your poverty; keep the appearance of not being in need.

241. **elli ixelli daru mah̲lula iji Salah̲ Gella yexralu fiha**

If you leave your house open, Salah Gella [a known and feared bandit] will come and defecate in it.

Always keep your door shut; you will be safer.

242. **elli ixunha sa'dha tqul rajli mesh̲ur**

The woman who has no luck in marriage says that her husband has been bewitched.

You always find excuses for your own shortcomings.

243. **elli jėk ustenjėk saqilu men âśak wefreślu men g̅tak**

When somebody comes to you and shows you respect, serve him your dinner and make his bed.

244. **elli kla karmusa xaraf**

He ate one fig and he thought the autumn had come.

A swallow doesn't make a spring.

245. **elli lbės jerteyla ba'd ârah yemśi uyetlafat urah**

When one wears a coat after he has been in rags, he walks and looks behind him [to see if people are noticing his new outfit].

246. **elli lemmettu ennemeyla fi âm yaklu ejmel fi śeffa**

What the ant has gathered in one year, the camel will eat in one mouthful.

One saves everything for years and the other (an heir) spends it very quickly.

247. **elli lesêtu ellefâ metsersib leẖbel ixaf**

After he was bitten by the snake, he is afraid of the rope.

A burned cat dreads the fire.

248. **elli ma ându la ẖnin la wali iâyet lelkelb ya xali**

He who has no relative or compassionate defender will call the dog "uncle."

One will accept help wherever one can get it, even from a dog.

249. **elli ma ându nar ma yetselefha mejjar**

If you don't have fire, don't borrow it from your neighbor.

Don't borrow even the necessities; do without.

250. **elli ma ându ṡahed ma ându din**

He who does not have a witness does not have a religion.

Exclamation of satisfaction when someone confirms what you say and bears testimony to your truthfulness.

251. **elli madxulu xmasi umaxruju sdasi tol ômru iqasi**

If his income is five and his expense is six, he will be in need all of his life.

Don't spend more than what you earn; deficit is very destructive.

252. **elli ma irodṡ ettar buh ẖmar**

He who does not take his revenge, his father is a donkey.

253. **elli ma ja ândek ma temṡilu**

Do not go to his house if he does not come to yours.

Relations can endure only if there is reciprocity; do not impose on others; show self-respect.

254. **elli ma lẖaqṡ elliya iqul mentna hiya**

If you don't reach the fat meat, you say it is rotten.

When you can't have something, you speak evil of it.

255. **elli ma qra ma dra**

One who has not studied cannot know.

Knowledge is acquired through hard study.

256. **elli matet omu ma tâwfu essayẖa**

He whose mother died will not be scared by the screaming and yelling.

When you get used to something bad, you become immune to it. It has no effect on you anymore.

257. **elli matet omu thèd fomu**

His mother died, his mouth was destroyed.

An orphan cannot enjoy talking or eating, or any other activity; the mother is the most precious thing in life.

258. **elli ma weldek ma ih̲on âlik**

He who did not give birth to you will not be compassionate and helpful.

Don't expect strangers to feel for you, or to rescue you from distress.

259. **elli ma ya'refś isalli iqul leh̲sira mâwja**

He who can't pray says the floor mat is crooked.

One always finds something else to blame for his own shortcomings.

260. **elli ma yedri igul sbul**

When one does not know, he will say "corn."

In corn fields, there are people whose duty is to yell to scare the birds. Sometimes, they are attacked and they yell for help. But people think it is still for the protection of the "corn."

Appearances can be misleading. When you see a poor man well-dressed and clean, you think he is rich.

261. **elli ma yeqraś la'quba ma ilu feddar sah̲eb**

He who does not foresee the bad end of things does not have a friend in the house.

Everybody avoids him because he is dangerous.

262. **elli ma yeśqa ma yelqa**

If you don't toil, you don't find.

263. **elli mektub fejbin lazem tśufu elâyn**

What is written on the forehead must be seen by the eye.

The mektub *is your destiny, your fate (literally, "what is written" by God). It is inevitable, it must happen, and the eye must see it come true. There is very little a man can do in this life. Everything is predetermined.*

264. **elli mestanes yakol mennek kif iśufek ijo'**

If someone is used to eating your food, when he sees you he gets hungry.

Dependence on others makes one lazy and greedy.

265. **elli mèś tqolu dniya qolu xud sa' śîr**

Instead of cursing someone, offer him a sack of barley.

It pays to be nice, to talk nicely, and be generous, rather than fight and curse.

266. **elli mḡoti bemta' ennas ôryan**

He who is covered with other people's clothes is naked.

Don't count on others, only on yourself.

267. **elli nẖotu taẖti xir men omi woxti**

What I put under me is better than my mother and my sister.

One prefers his wife to his mother and sister.

268. **elli nwah Haman mẖah Mordexay**

What Haman planned, Mordecai foiled.

When we foil an attempt or a plot to harm us, and when the plotter gets the punishment he intended for his victims.

269. **elli ôjbu suqlarba' ikamal suqlexmis**

If you liked the Wednesday market [or the city by that name], you will visit the Thursday market [or the city by that name].

If one enjoys a certain activity (good or bad), he keeps doing it.

270. **elli qaslu wednu elẖakem ma yetsamaś âkrut**

He whose ear was cut by the government cannot be called a rascal.

There is no shame in being punished by the government, or the legal authorities.

271. **elli sab errah̲a felahbal aś h̲ajtu belâqal**

If one can find comfort in madness, who needs reason?

If you find reward for doing nothing, why work hard?

272. **elli śenêt harbet welli fezêt śedduha**

The woman who committed adultery escaped and the one who yelled got caught.

The guilty go unpunished and the innocent pay for the crimes of the guilty.

273. **elli śenêt tkamal leyletha**

If a woman commits adultery, let her finish her night.

Once you have committed a sin, or any bad action, you might as well enjoy it to the end.

274. **elli serwalu melh̲alfa ma yoqrobś lennar**

If your trousers are made of straw, don't come close to the fire.

One must be extra careful when one is vulnerable.

275. **elli ta'mel yeddu yeh̲mel qalbu**

What your hand will do, your heart will suffer.

You are responsible for your own acts.

276. **elli telqah rakeb âla xośba qolu mella jwèd**

If you see someone riding a log, tell him what a beautiful horse.

Do not antagonize people, let them enjoy their own fantasies.

277. **elli texdmu tiû welli terhnu biû**

Obey those you serve, and sell what you pawn [give as collateral for a loan].

The first part of this proverb is practical: otherwise you lose your job. The second part reflects the sad fact that the borrower, mainly the peasant, is unable to repay his loan on time, and thus forfeits his collateral, usually jewelry. The advice is: better to sell the jewelry than mortgage it. The result is that you will get more money and not borrow any more, because borrowing is a ruinous activity.

278. **elli th̲ab tenkih oskot âlih uxalih**

If you want to make him angry, let him talk and don't respond.

279. **elli tqolu ya sidi ibiêk feddalal**

If you call someone "master," he will sell you at an auction.

If you let yourself be exploited, people will take advantage of you.

280. **elli ttalaqha ma twariha dar buha**

When you divorce your wife, don't show her her father's house.

When you put an end to some troublesome situation (a bad marriage, a partnership), don't look back, don't try to find what happened to the other party, don't give advice. Just forget it.

281. **elli xala xliftu ma matś**

He who has left an heir did not die.

This stresses the importance of having children, especially males, who will continue the name and traditions of the family.

282. **elli xalfuh ejdud yefniuh elqrud**

What was left by the parents will be finished by the monkeys.

It is silly to leave an inheritance; somebody else, stranger to the family, will enjoy it.

283. **elli yadrbek belẖjar adrbu belxobz, enti xobzek iwellilek uhuwa ẖajru iwellilu**

If someone hits you with a stone, hit him with bread; your bread will return to you and his stone will return to him.

284. **elli yahbet lelâsa yakol bśabû**

If one is subjected to beating [or whipping], let him have it in abundance.

This is against half-measures; even bad things, like whipping, should be given in serious quantity, otherwise they will not be effective as punishment.

285. **elli yahrob men elmeks welkra yahrob melbey' weśra**

If you flee from taxes and rent, you flee from selling and buying.

If you want to do business, you must put up with expenses such as rent, taxes . . .

286. **elli yakol âdeymet errebi yexraha flales**

The person who eats the rabbi's egg will excrete chicks.

If you accept something from the rabbi (the clergy in general), you will have to return it tenfold. Clergymen take much more than they give.

287. **elli yakol men qowtek yestana fi mowtek**

He who feeds on you is waiting for your death.

Dependency makes people lazy, selfish, and cruel.

288. **elli yakol zra' ennas ixali zarû âtniya**

He who eats other people's grain leaves his grain in the street.

If you fool around with other women, your wife will be vulnerable because she might decide to take her revenge for your cheating, or because other men will find it easier to approach her.

289. **elli ya'mel bidu ma ikidu**

When one is the cause of his problems, he should be responsible.

Don't blame others for your own shortcomings.

290. **elli ya'mel elxeyr ma iśawer**

He who does a good deed does not ask for permission to do it.

Everybody would like to benefit from a good deed.

291. **elli ya'mel gerba âla dahru toqtor**

If you carry a goatskin bag on your head, it will drip on your back.

Everybody is responsible for his own acts, and must pay for his mistakes.

292. **elli ya'ref dar luba wijiha imut fiha men g̅eyr a'mor**

He who knows that the house is infected with pestilence and still enters it will die in it before his age.

If you do something risky deliberately and knowingly, or after you have been warned, you will suffer the tragic consequences, and will have only yourself to blame.

293. **elli yasbar inal**

With patience, you will succeed.

294. **elli ya'tik h̲bel ketfu bih**

If he gives you a rope, tie him with it.

If one is so dumb as to give you his weapon, or his possessions, he is the loser; don't have pity on him.

295. **elli ya'ti rezqu fi h̲yètu, tlab rabi ma g̅atu**

He who gives away his possessions while he is alive, God will not respond to his prayers.

Do not give anything (to your children, mainly) in your

lifetime; you will lose their respect and become destitute; they will abandon you; and if you complain to God, he will not answer you. This stresses the ingratitude of children.

296. **elli yaxod men dar sḡira, ida ma yakol triẖa ibèt felâra**

He who marries into a poor family, if he is not beaten he will sleep without a cover.

Better marry into a rich family.

297. **elli yaxod ôla biha mèt**

If you marry a log, you die with it.

Whatever you get as a bride, that's for life, and you deserve it.

298. **elli yaxod omna huwa buna**

He who takes our mother is our father.

We must submit to the strong and the powerful; if he is strong enough to take our mother, he deserves to be our father. A different interpretation: We must love and respect our mother's new husband because we love her; the friend of our friend is our friend.

299. **elli yebni taẖuna ya'melha dendèn**

He who builds a mill [to grind grain] must also have a bell.

It is not enough to have a business; you must advertise it. This is a call for perfection.

300. **elli yelqa dar xir men dar buh yeđî âla dar buh belxla**

If one finds a house better than his father's house, he will curse his father's house and wish its destruction.

Personal interest is stronger than family ties.

301. **elli yesker ma yettajer**

If you drink, don't become a merchant.

Because you will be unable to manage the business, and you will lose everything.

302. **elli yesma' yefza' welli itol yahrob**

He who learns about it will be terrified, and he who sees it will run away.

Sarcastic: this is in response to someone who tells you trivialities and gives them the importance of a very serious matter.

303. **elli yesraq ebra yesraq bagra**

He who steals a needle will steal a cow.

One should educate one's children never to take anything that does not belong to them.

304. **elli yesraq yeḡleb elli iẖaẖi**

The thief will always beat the guard.

However you strengthen the guard, there will always be thieves who will overcome it.

305. **elli yestana xir melli yetmana**

It is better to wait patiently [for something real and tangible] than to rush into something with illusions.

306. **elli yetfakar ras malu idux**

If you remember your capital, you will get a headache.

When you find yourself embroiled in a bad deal, you get a headache just thinking about your investment in it. Think before you act.

307. **elli yetkel âla dar elôrs ibat bla âśa**

If you count on the wedding feast, you will go to sleep without dinner.

Don't rely on others, count only on yourself; nobody will give you anything; no free lunch.

308. **elli yetkel âlih ibèt bla âśa**

If you count on him, you will go to sleep without dinner.

He is absolutely unreliable, you can't trust his promises, he will let you down; take care of yourself!

309. **elli yetkel âlulad ikarkru elwėd**

He who counts on his children will be dragged by the river.

Don't rely on your children to care for you in your old days. Save for a rainy day.

310. **elli yezra' eśśar yoẖsod enndama**

If you sow evil, you will reap regret.

311. **elli yezra' eśśowk iẖir fi ẖsadu**

When one sows thorns, he will have a problem harvesting.

It is easy to cause trouble, but much more difficult to get out of it.

312. **elli yobzoq lesqaf terja' bazqtu ala wejju**

When one spits on the ceiling, his spittle returns to him.

When you attack or slander someone higher than you, you hurt yourself.

313. **elli yofdel feddar yeddi lekra**

The one who remains in the house will pay the rent.

Everybody is leaving, everyone for himself; the last ones will suffer.

314. **elli yoẖleflek xaf mennek ula dėrėk**

If one swears to you, either he is afraid of you or he is kind to you.

When you are honest, you need not swear (by God).

315. **elli yohrob menėk ma tejriś urah**

If somebody flees from you, don't run after him.

Do not seek the company or the friendship of those who try to avoid you.

316. **elli yoh̲sob âśatu ibat bla âśa**

If you count the cost of your dinner, you will go to bed hungry.

Whatever is necessary to subsist, do it regardless of cost.

317. **elli yoktor malu tesḡar daru uteśwam âyalu**

He whose wealth increases, his house becomes smaller and his wife becomes very bad.

Yes, because he will need a bigger house and his wife will make more demands for new expenses and pleasures.

318. **elli yoktor malu yoktor ahbalu**

When your wealth increases your craziness increases.

Money is a bad master; it can be harmful.

319. **elloz elmor la yenfa' ula idor**

Bitter almonds can do no good and no harm.

This applies to dull people who have nothing to say: they are not harmful, nor are they enjoyable.

320. **ellula smèn, ettanya âsal, wettalta zeft uqotran**

The first is cream, the second is honey, and the third is coal-tar.

When you repeat even a good thing, it will become bad.

321. **elma elli mèśi lessedra lezzeytuna ula bih**

The water that goes to the lotus tree had better go to the olive tree.

Don't waste resources; spend only for a profitable purpose.

322. **elmaǵruq iśed fi smara**

The person who is drowning will hold onto a twig.

In desperate situations, any help is welcome; any remedy should be tried.

323. **elmaśquq welmanqub welli tayaẖ qaû**

The cracked, the full of holes, and the bottomless.

This describes pots, pans, and dishes. In the figurative, it refers to people of the lowest kind, or to friends of ill-repute, a gang of thugs.

324. **elmazlut felqafla motman**

The poor man has nothing to fear from the brigands.

When you have nothing to lose, you are safe.

325. **elmedxul iâlmek elmexruj**

The income should teach you the expense.

Don't spend more than you earn.

326. **elmelẖ ma idawed**

The salt never gets worms.

A man who is strong, morally, or physically, cannot be broken or corrupted.

327. **elmenbub âla rasu riśa**

The guilty person has a feather on his head.

Story: after a crime was committed, nobody confessed. A smart judge gathered all the suspects and said, "I know who the criminal is; the criminal has a feather on his head." One of the suspects put his hand on his head, and the judge said: "You are the criminal." The man confessed. If the shoe fits . . .

328. **elmenbuba maẖbuba walu tkun marûba**

A woman of ill repute is loved even if she is ugly.

A loose woman will always find a man for a short encounter even if she is unattractive.

329. **elme'za mkarkarha elwėd wiya tqul elâm gatar matar**

The goat was being carried away by the torrents, and she said: "What a blessed year!" [full of rain].

Applies to a situation when a person is in danger and not only unaware of it but praising the cause of the danger. Example: the house is burning and somebody is inside enjoying the warmth.

330. **elmh̲aba terkeb âla ûd naśef**

Love can grow even on a dry stick.

If there is love, one can achieve the impossible.

331. **elmh̲aba welh̲adba mafihom mayetxaba**

Love and hump cannot be hidden.

The hump is obvious, and love shows on your face and from your behavior. Don't try to lie about it.

332. **elmnaqla medbala walu ikunu âruśha felma**

A transplanted plant will fade away even if its roots are in water.

A person who emigrates to another country is unhappy even if he has made a fortune.

333. **elmot lazma wela'dab âlaś**

Death is unavoidable, so why suffer.

334. **elmot maâ ejmaâ xlaâ**

Death in company is a vacation.

If the same catastrophe befalls everyone, it is more bearable. Misery loves company.

335. **elmot sotra men eddheb**

Death covers better than gold.

When a dishonored person dies, the dishonor dies with him.

336. **elmra ida sallat znat**

The woman who has prayed has committed adultery.

The hypocrites hide their ugly behavior, and put on an appearance of holiness and integrity.

337. **elmra texli elmra tâmar; elmra tfaraẖ elmra tqaraẖ**

The wife destroys, the wife brings prosperity; the wife makes you happy, the wife makes you sad.

Everything depends on the wife; she is the cause of success and happiness, or of failure and sorrow.

338. **elmxobi âjiran mśum**

What is hidden from the neighbor is bad.

First, you can't hide anything from your neighbors; sooner or later, they will know; and until then, they will think your secret is worse than it actually is.

339. **el om ma tetbadal belxala**

You cannot replace a mother with an aunt [mother's sister].

The mother is irreplaceable.

340. **el om śelba welbu qarus yetla' luled ẖay neggez**

The mother is a bass, the father is a perch, the son will be neither this nor that [maybe both].

We inherit the characteristics of our genitors and behave accordingly.

What do you expect of him? Look at his parents.

341. **elôtśan irum lelẖma**

A thirsty person will consent [to drink] polluted water.

342. **elôtśan ma tzafarlu wejjuân ma tqolu kul**

Don't whistle to the thirsty [and ask them to drink], and don't tell the hungry to eat.

Everybody knows what he needs, and will take care of himself; don't interfere.

343. **elqad qad elfula welẖos ẖos elḡula**

Small like a pea, but with the voice of an ogre.

Appearance can be misleading; don't misjudge a person on account of his size.

344. **elqaẖba tèbet nofs nhar qalet nhar mśum âl qẖab**

The whore repented for half a day and became jealous of the other whores.

Money has a powerful force of temptation to make you do immoral things.

345. **elqalb ida tġayar elwej ya'ti xbara**

If the heart is hurt, the face will show.

346. **elqalb ma iẖab kèn elli iẖabu**

The heart loves only those who love it.

Love is reciprocal, and one feels other people's love instinctively.

347. **elqard ma idaya'ś elfula**

The monkey will not lose the [fava] bean.

No one will refuse anything good, or let a good opportunity pass him by.

348. **elquwa leddo'f terja'**

Strong today, weak tomorrow.

349. **elqwi dèrih ulè bèrih ulè oskot âlih uxalih**

The powerful person, you must either be nice to him, or avoid him, or let him talk without answering him.

350. **elûd elli rabeyt bih nekweyt**

The branch which I raised, I was burned by it.

The water says: I nourished the branch and now, they made fire with it, and the fire is burning me (i.e. boiling water). This applies to someone who is threatened, or hurt, by his children or by people he has helped and nurtured for a long period (Caesar to Brutus, for example: "Et tu, Brute!"). It is used in general as a complaint against ingratitude.

351. **elwarda tuled ś̀awka weś̀awka tuled warda**

From the rose comes a thorn, and from the thorn comes a rose.

Anti-genetic precept: you never know what your children will be like; the laws of heredity do not apply.

352. **elxat âla ewlu**

Handwriting is learned at a young age.

When you learn something, you must learn it properly from the beginning. It is difficult to get rid of bad habits.

353. **elxeyr ida ma trodu ôdu**

If you cannot return a service rendered to you, or a good deed, or a favor, you should at least count it; that is, remember it and acknowledge it.

354. **elxlè yexli wela'jul tdur**

The desert is empty and the calves are running around.

Total desolation, no living soul, even the calves are running desperately to find some grass, but in vain.

355. **elyebra ma tânedś elleś́fa**

The needle cannot compete with the awl.

The weak should not fight the strong; the ignorant should not argue with the learned.

356. **elyed etwila telh̲aq elârjun**

The long arm reaches the bunch [of dates or other fruits].

If you are strong, or if you have good connections, you can get what you want.

357. **elyom ẖbab uḡodwa qtates weklab**

Today friends, tomorrow cats and dogs.

Friendship does not last.

358. **emlaha belxenfus utâda qodam âduk belbus**

Fill it [your belly] with cockroaches, and show off to your enemy with clothes.

It is more important to buy clothes than food, because your peers will judge you only by your clothes which they can see, and not by what you eat, which you can do behind closed doors.

359. **emśi belmdasa ẖata tujed essabat**

Wear cloth sandals until you can afford real shoes.

Content yourself with little until you can improve. Don't beg others to give you anything.

360. **ennefxa wetternana wetterma elôryana**

Boasting and bragging and the buttocks are bare.

People who have nothing to show for but are constantly bragging.

361. **ensa etma' yensak elfqar**

Forget the greed, and poverty will forget you.

Greedy people are never satisfied, therefore they always think they are poor.

362. **ensib ômru ma iwelli ẖbib**

The son-in-law will never become a friend.

363. **enti amir wana amir weśkun isuq elẖmir**

You are a prince and I am a prince, and who will lead the donkeys.

The job must be done, whether we like it or not; no job is demeaning.

364. **enwi ennaqs tbėt felkmal**

Be suspicious, and you will sleep in safety.

It is better to err on the side of excess of suspicion and caution than be caught unaware for lack of suspicion.

365. **errebh welxsara fard ṡkara**

Gain and loss are in the same bag.

In business you can't always win; you must accept loss sometimes. Or: he lives without counting income and expense.

366. **errjal qûd wennsa qûd aṡ ikun fi ulad leqrud**

If the men sit idle and the women sit idle, what will happen to the children?

One must work, not be lazy.

367. **erxis ḡali welḡali rxis**

Cheap is expensive and expensive is cheap.

You get what you pay for.

368. **eṡ ėjbek fezman ella tolu**

What quality do you like in time? Its length.

Vengeance can wait, time never ends; one day you will take your revenge.

369. **es-el elmujarab uma tes-elṡ tbib**

Ask the experienced person, and don't ask a physician.

Experience is better than science; practice is better than theory.

370. **eṡ ilezzek men elmor ken amar mennu**

What is stronger than bitter? More bitter.

Resign to your fate, because it could be worse.

371. ès iqul elmiyet qodam ḡusalu!

What can the corpse say to his washers!

This is said about a person who is totally helpless, such as a prisoner being tortured, or somebody completely dependent on somebody else. What can he say, or do? Nothing.

372. ès iqul ettajer âla bdayû!

What will the merchant say about his merchandise!

Nobody will speak evil of himself or his family; no one will incriminate himself.

373. eś iśaba' ejmel mettifaf

The camel will not be satisfied with small leaves.

This is not a real solution to the problem; this is only a band-aid; or, this is very little and no help at all.

374. eś iwasal ḡorbti lehli

Who will tell my family about my exile?

Nobody will hear about me when I am in distress.

375. eś ixallas eśśowk melkonteyl!

What will separate the thorns from the silver threads!

How to keep the good things and throw out the bad!

376. esqi eddalia yekber elânqud

Water the vine, the bunch of grapes will be bigger.

Nurture (education) is very important.

377. essanâ teḡni âl msasia wettijara tqata' slasel elfqar

Manual labor, even skilled, is better only than begging, but business breaks the chains of poverty.

378. eśśayb welâyb

Old age and vice!

These two don't go together.

379. **eśśba' ma fih foxra wejjo' ma fih âr**

There is no pride in having enough to eat and no shame in being hungry.

380. **eśśebeyk elli yodxol mennu erriẖ sakru westriẖ**

The window that lets the wind in, close it and stop worrying.

If you have a problem that is bothering you, solve it and get rid of it without delay.

381. **eśśebka tqul lelḡorbal mowsa' âynek ya herwal**

The net telling the sieve how wide its eyes are.

One sees faults and defects in others, and doesn't see the same in himself.

382. **eśśen śen werkiz rkiz**

What is strong is strong, and what is weak is weak.

Accurate talk, precise. You can count on that person; he knows what he is talking about.

383. **eśśhar elli mafih ennfiâ ma tôdlu ayam**

The month that brings no benefit, don't count its days.

Don't waste your time doing things that are not profitable.

384. **esskat men errda**

Silence means acquiescence.

If you don't object to something, you are in agreement, and you will forfeit your right to complain.

385. **essnin lemśuma iwaryuk lujuh leẖrof**

Bad years will show you bad faces.

When there is no crop, everybody comes to ask you for help, for a loan.

386. **eśśra bsidi ben âbas welbey' belmènubiya**

When you buy, you have to invoke the saints, and when

you sell, you need a musical band.

It is not easy to find what you need to buy, and it is very difficult to find a buyer for what you want to sell.

387. **essuf tetba' berzana**

The wool is sold with patience.

The wool business has its seasons; you must be patient and wait for the good selling time.

Don't rush into anything; wait for the opportune moment.

388. **estana ya djaja h̲ata ijik elqamh̲ men baja**

Wait, little chicken, until the grains come from Baja.

Baja is in grain-producing country. The chickens that feed on grain are exhorted to wait patiently. This proverb is used when somebody is asked to be patient, waiting for something that could come (like the grain from Baja), but usually never comes.

389. **eś ya'mlu yeddeya mâ xoddeya**

What can my hands do with my cheeks?

I am between two relatives or two friends who had a fight. I love both of them and don't know what to do.

390. **etâda âla wèd harhar umatetâdaś âla wèd saket**

Cross a turbulent river and don't cross a quiet one.

Beware of people who appear to be quiet; don't trust their appearance, they may fool you.

391. **etâm elfom testh̲i elâyn**

Feed the mouth, and the eye will be respectful.

A gift (or bribe) will help you get what you want.

392. **etâmu yetqawa uma ikunlek g̅rim ella huwa**

Feed him, he will be strong, and will become your worst enemy.

You may be the victim of your good deeds.

393. **etbennen qbel ma tkennen**

Enjoy yourself before you bring a daughter-in-law to your mother.

Enjoy yourself as long as you are a bachelor.

394. **etelha ya rajel bexrak**

Take care of your own excrements, man!

Don't interfere in other people's problems, take care of your own.

395. **etfina wensib bensib**

A Jewish sabbath meal [that has simmered on slow heat all of Friday night], and a son-in-law, are a matter of luck.

You will never know what your daughter will bring you as a son-in-law.

396. **etḡada wetmada walu ikunu darjeyn, etâśa wetmaśa walu ikunu khatuteyn**

After lunch, take a nap even for a few minutes; after dinner, take a walk even for a few steps.

397. **etla' ya far men elḡar**

Get out of the hole, mouse.

Don't ask someone to do something to endanger himself.

398. **ètriẖa welmeẖsuda ida fetu mètu**

A beating you received and a dirty trick played on you, if they are over, they are dead.

If you have been victimized, there is no need to keep repeating the story to others; forget about the past.

399. **ettaś ula la'ma**

Better to see very little than be totally blind.

Half a loaf is better than no loaf.

400. **etterka mśèt kif la'sel fesswaba'**

Inherited wealth disappears like honey through the fingers.

You respect only what you have worked for; what you herit will melt away very fast.

401. **ettolba tegni ama txellef elâr**

Begging can make you rich, but will leave dishonor.

402. **ettunsia kelmetha fi fomha wennablia h̲ata tśawer omha**

The girl from Tunis has the word ready in her mouth; the girl from Nabel must wait until she consults with her mother.

Difference between people from the capital and from the provinces; people are more timid and less educated in the provinces.

403. **ewlethem qh̲ab wa'qabhem dgagez**

They start as whores and end up as fortune tellers.

When they can no longer sell their physical advantages (youth and beauty), they try another way to extort money. It is always the same game, only the means have changed.

404. **exdem âla ârdek h̲ata yetsama wida yetsama yexdem âlik**

Work on your reputation until it is established; when it is established, it will work for you.

405. **exdem bqafsi uh̲aseb elbatal**

Work for a penny and compete with the idle.

Only idle people will have no money; if you work, for whatever wages, you will still fare better than the unemployed.

406. **exdem tekdem, oqôd tendem**

Work, and you will bite; sit, and you will regret.

Idleness is the source of all evil.

407. **exdem ya âbdi wana nînek**

Work, my servant, and I will help you.

Don't rely on outside help; do your work, help yourself. God helps those who help themselves.

408. **exdem ya bu lulad uxabi lkobrok śweya**

Work, father of children, and save something for your old age.

Don't count on your children to support you when you are old.

409. **exdem ya taês bsa'd erraqed wennaês**

Work, poor guy, for the benefit of the sleepers and the lazy.

Some people work hard so that others can enjoy rest and leisure.

410. **exta rasi wadrab**

Spare my head and hit.

As long as I am not hurt, I don't mind what you do to others. Men are selfish.

411. **èynek mizanek**

Your eye is your scale.

Use your own judgment; by seeing something, you will be able to evaluate it.

412. **èyneyn lemh̲aba melbîd ibènu**

The eyes of love can be distinguished from afar.

You can't hide your love, your eyes will express it.

413. **ezzafzif uqalet elâsal**

Too much humming and too little honey.

Too much noise (boasting and bragging) but no tangible results.

414. **ezzeyn huwa zeyn elfâyel**

Beauty is in the character.

Character and personality are more important than physical beauty.

415. **ezzeyn ixelli xtutu wesmen ixelli jludu**

Beauty will leave its trace, and obesity will leave its skin.

You can never hide anything; it will eventually show.

416. **ezzman elma'kus ednabi twelli rus**

In crooked times, the tails become heads.

It is the sign of bad times when the ignorant lead the educated, the students their teachers, the children their parents, etc. . . .

417. **fard fares ma itayar g̃obeyra**

One horseman does not make much dust.

The strength is in the numbers; one person alone cannot do much.

418. **far inetten xabya**

A mouse will foul a jar.

Earthenware jars are usually filled with oil or other kinds of preserved food; a mouse falling into a jar can ruin the whole thing. In the figurative: one member of a family (or group) can destroy its reputation by his bad conduct.

419. **fedalma kol mra gamra**

In the dark, all women are moons.

When you don't see something, you can't discover its defects. In the dark, all cats are gray.

420. **fedayqa ibanu leẖbab**

Friends are recognized in times of stress.

A friend in need is a friend indeed.

421. **felwej mraya ufelqfa zag̅aya**

In your presence, a mirror; in your absence, a sting.

A two-faced hypocrite.

422. **fenèg uzid kol yom sa'd jdid**

Be as ugly as you can, everyday a new luck [applies to girls at puberty].

However ugly you may be, if you are lucky, you will be very successful with men.

423. **fi bled elârjin a'mel nefsek a'raj**

In the land of the lame, pretend to be lame.

In Rome, do as the Romans. Don't be different from the group, especially when you are a guest.

424. **fi h̲yatu śtha besra, fi motu âlqulu ârjun**

When he was alive, he craved for a date; when he died, they gave him a bunch of dates.

He was mistreated and abandoned all his life; when he died, they praised him.

425. **fi sanêt buk ma yeg̅lbuk**

In the trade of your father, no one can surpass you.

Expertise comes from practice.

426. **frayda ulqat oxtha**

One of a pair found the other.

They look alike, like two peas in a pod, or: birds of a feather flock together.

427. **fula umaqsuma âla tneyn**

A pea divided in two.

They look alike, like two peas in a pod.

428. **fxarna la'rusa telêt ẖobla**

We praised the bride, and she was found pregnant.

You brag about something and the truth crudely explodes in your face.

429. **ḡaltet elqalil sarqa usarqet elḡni ḡalta**

The error of the poor is a theft, the theft of the rich is an error.

Double standard; the rich can do anything and get away with it.

430. **ẖabni mẖabet xuk uẖasebni ẖsab âduk**

Love me as if I were your brother and do your accounts with me as if I were your enemy.

One must separate business from sentiment; business is business; short reckonings make long friends.

431. **hada muś hemmek, hemmek fi ras âmek**

This is not your problem; your problems are taken care of by your uncle.

Don't worry, somebody is doing that for you.

432. **ẖadar essarj welẖsan mazal fi kerś omu**

He prepared the harness, and the horse is still in his mother's belly.

Don't put the cart before the horse; or, don't count your chickens before they are hatched.

433. **ẖadar leẖsira qbel ejjama'**

He prepared the prayer mat before the mosque [was built].

He put the cart before the horse.

434. **ẖad ma lqaha kif elli śtaha**

Nobody found it the way he wished it to be.

One never gets what he desires.

435. **ẖajra men yed leẖbib tefaẖa**

A stone from the hands of a friend is an apple.

We can easily accept reproaches, or even some harm, from a friend. Friends should not take offense from each other.

436. **ẖamar wejek minuta wala toqôd ẖzin elâm kolu**

Blush one minute rather than suffer for the whole year.

It is better to say (or do) something unpleasant now than to keep it inside and be bothered by it for a long time.

437. **ẖart la'jul ma ikabar nwader**

The ploughing of the calves will not increase the haystacks.

The work (or help) of weak people does not add very much to the results.

438. **ẖata fi qabru yetaẖraq**

Even in his grave, he is being burned.

They say evil of him even after he is dead and buried; they continue to hit him after he is down. Flogging a dead horse.

439. **ẖata tuled wiîśelha**

Until she gives birth and the baby survives!

Don't make plans when there are a lot of ifs. Don't count your chickens before they are hatched.

440. **ẖata yed elqatusa tâwen**

Even the hand of the cat can help.

Do not underestimate small things; they add up.

441. **ẖaya taẖt etben**

Like a serpent under the straw.

Sneaky; underhanded; treacherous.

442. **hay hay ya sayem fi romdan**

Boo him, the one who fasts in Ramadan.

You are supposed to fast during the month of Ramadan, if you are a Moslem. Here, sarcasm: the one who observes religion, morality, law, manners, deserves to be booed; no more respect for the righteous; on the contrary, they are despised.

443. **ẖayt ermal ma tâlih, yekber witiẖ sèsha; farx ezzna ma trabih, yekber uyerja' lnèsha**

Don't erect a high building on sand foundations, it will crumble after some time; don't raise an illegitimate child, he will grow up and become like his natural progenitors.

444. **ẖbibek huwa maktubek**

Your friend is your pocket.

Don't rely on others, only on yourself; without money, you have no friends.

445. **hèdi sekkina bwejheyn**

This is a double-edged knife.

You can't have it both ways.

446. **ẖlof âdar dxal lelâtba, ẖlof âlẖam śrab elmarqa**

He swore not to come to the house [but] he passed the threshold; he swore [not to eat] meat [but] he drank its broth.

He is not a man of his word.

447. **ẖmura felwej ula ḡossa felqalb**

Better blush than keep the burden in your heart.

It is healthier to say what you think even if it is embarrassing than to suffer in silence.

448. **ẖolfet el-ard mâ essma la tetxaba la sarqa la zna**

Heaven and earth have sworn that stealing and whoring can never be hidden.

All wrongdoers will eventually get caught; nothing can remain secret forever.

449. **ẖot âla botnek betixa sayfi**

Put in your belly a summer melon.

A summer melon is always good, sweet, juicy. Used seriously, this means: "You can count on me." Sarcastically, it means the opposite.

450. **ẖot nefsek mâ ennoxala iferfšek edjaj**

Put yourself with the chicken food, you will be messed up by the chicken.

If you go to places of ill repute, you may end up as a victim of crimes; stay away from dubious people and places.

451. **ẖšem ejjerbi men nsibtu ḡata wejju âra msibtu**

The Djerbian was embarrassed in front of his mother-in-law; he covered his face and uncovered his private parts. [Djerba is a city in Tunisia.]

You fix something on one side and make it worse on another.

452. **ẖut yakol ẖut uqlil ejjehd imut**

Fish eat fish, and the weak will die.

It is a dog-eat-dog world; only the strong will survive.

453. **huwa ubuh tšerku mšaw lessuq tfarqu**

He and his father became partners; they went to the market and separated.

Partnership is not good, especially between family members.

454. **iâned elbassasin blaši termeyn**

He wants to fart like the others but he has no behind.

One cannot do everything other people do; one must know his limitations.

455. **ibi' elqard uyetmenyek âli yeśrih**

He sells the monkey and makes fun of the buyer.

He cheats you and laughs at you that you could be so easily duped.

456. **ibos ubotnu farġa**

He farts and his belly is empty.

He talks without knowing what he is saying; he boasts of something he doesn't have.

457. **ibus fom yensa fom**

He kisses a mouth and forgets a mouth.

He finds a new friend, and forgets the old ones; he is unreliable.

458. **ida âdak jarek bèdèl darek**

If your neighbor surpasses you [in wealth], move out.

One must keep up with the Joneses.

459. **ida ba'bus elkelb igata'ni ma themniś ntuntu**

If the tail of the dog can save me, I don't care about its stench.

Accept help from wherever it comes; don't be choosy.

460. **ida bentek feznaqi śuf ârdek ida baqi**

If your daughter is in the streets, check your honor to see if it is still there.

Daughters of good families should never wander in the streets, but should stay home to protect their virtue and the family's honor.

461. **ida da<u>h</u>ku ma bqalhemś âlaś yebkiw**

If they laughed, there is nothing left to cry about.

Because they have cried about everything, there is no happiness whatsoever.

Putting on a good face to a bad situation.

462. **ida elqatus welfar yetsalẖu ẖata leẖma welârusa yetsamẖu**

If the cat and the mouse could make peace, then the bride and the mother-in-law will forgive each other.

The universal antagonism between bride and mother-in-law.

463. **ida ennar fi dar jarek, ẖadar elma fi darek**

If the fire is in your neighbor's house, prepare water in your house.

What is happening to others can happen to you too; don't wait until it is too late.

464. **ida enti kasru ana natfu**

If you break it, I smash it.

If you spend money, I can do worse; if you act irresponsibly, I will do worse.

465. **ida enti tbelleyt ana tẖalleyt**

You only got wet; I was completely ruined.

That's what a paper picture told its frame when they fell into water. What happened to you is nothing compared to what happened to me.

466. **ida enwaẖ bettolba la yarẖam elli mèt**

If mourning must be requested, let the dead people be cursed.

Mourning and, in general, feelings, must be sincere and spontaneous, not performed on command.

467. **ida fètek elklèm qul sma't wida fètek ettâm qul śba't**

If you couldn't hear what was said, say "I heard," and if you are late for dinner, say "I ate."

Don't impose on others; don't be a burden; don't ask them to repeat what you didn't hear or to cook something special for you because you came after dinner.

468. **ida g̃ab elmèdeb mada ya'mlu latfal**

When the teacher is away, [who knows] what pupils will do.

When the cat is away, the mice will play.

469. **ida g̃ab ezzeyn h̲adret hiya**

If beauty is absent, here she comes.

She thinks she is very beautiful, but in fact she is ugly.

470. **ida h̲abek elhalal bekmalu ès̀ ândek fenjum ida malu**

If the full moon loves you, why worry about the stars?

If you have the most important thing, be happy, count your blessings, and forget about everything else.

471. **ida h̲abuk ennsa ibeytuk fedfa, ida kerhuk ibeytuk felâra**

If the women like you, you will sleep in a warm bed; if they hate you, you will freeze without cover.

472. **ida h̲abuk s̀rif iredduk; ida kerhuk yenkru omok ubuk**

If they like you, they make you a noble; if they hate you, they will forget your mother and father.

It's not what you are really worth but how people feel about you that counts.

473. **ida h̲ajtek belkelb qolu ya sidi**

If you need anything from a dog, call him master.

In order to achieve your goals, bow to those you need and flatter them even if they are despicable.

474. **ida jèt tjibha s̀a'ra, ida ms̀èt tqata' eslasel**

When there is luck, one hair is enough; when there is no luck, even iron chains will break.

475. **ida kber śayeb eddar uqalet menu ennfiâ, yotlob âla śarbet elma, yaxod âliha ujiâ**

When the man in the house gets older and his usefulness diminishes, he asks for a drink of water and meets with a painful silence.

A warning to parents to save for their old days and not to become dependent on their children.

476. **ida kèn sa'dek âdidek mâd sayer elwaqt dima, armi âsatek men yeddek mâwja tji mostqima**

If luck is with you, you will always have it good; throw your stick from your hand, even if it is crooked, it will come out straight.

Everything is a matter of luck, regardless of what you do.

477. **ida lqeyt ezzehw wettob la tbeddelha la beśqa la betto'b**

If you found joy and perfection, don't change it for toil and hardship.

Be content with what you have, because a change may be worse.

478. **ida ma ta'mel elxeyr ma ijik eśśar**

If you don't do favors, you will not suffer from troubles.

People are ungrateful, and sometimes return bad for good.

479. **ida nesẖek elârbi nofs ennsiẖa leyh**

If the bedouin gives you a piece of advice, half the advice is for him.

Everyone looks after his own interest.

480. **ida ôjbok roxsu lawaẖ fessuq nofsu**

If you are attracted by cheap merchandise, you will throw half of it while you are still in the market.

You get what you pay for; there is no free lunch.

481. **ida qayma elâdma tfagas âl watad, ida raqda elkelb iśewel âl asad**

If there is luck, the egg will hatch on a stake; if there is no luck, the dog will piss on the lion.

Luck is everything.

482. **ida rayeskom a'ma èś tkun âqubetkom**

If your chief is blind, what would be your end!

What would be your punishment? Who knows what lies in store for you when you have a bad leader.

483. **ida rayt na'ś metôdi, qul hekka na'śi**

If you see a coffin at a funeral, say mine will be the same.

Everybody will die.

484. **ida sah̲bek âsal ma telh̲suś bkolu**

If your friend is honey, don't lick him thoroughly.

Don't abuse your benefactors; don't take advantage of a person who is kind and generous to you.

485. **ida śba' elbnadem kfar**

If a man is full [of food], he will forget God.

Man is ungrateful and forgets his benefactor.

486. **ida śebêt elkerś tqul lerras ḡani**

If the belly is full, it will tell the head to sing.

One can never be happy on an empty stomach.

487. **ida sellem âlik elârbi tuh̲el fi âśah**

If the bedouin greets you, you may be stuck with his dinner.

Beware of nice words and appearances; they may cost you, you may be duped.

488. **ida tah̲et elbagra mada yah̲dru men skaken**

When the cow falls, all the knives are ready.

As long as you are strong, you are respected and feared; but if you fall, everybody will attack you as an easy prey and claim his share of the spoils.

489. **ida tẖab tadrab martek katafha**

If you want to beat your wife, tie her.

The best punishment you can inflict on your wife is to tie her down with children.

490. **ida tẖab tesraq somâ ẖadrelha bir**

If you want to steal a tower, prepare a well for it.

If you don't know how to hide the stolen merchandise, don't steal. One must foresee the consequences of one's acts.

491. **ida tneyn metâśrin eddrak âla waẖed**

If you see two people living in harmony, one of them is suffering from the burden.

Most relationships are based on dominance and exploitation, not on real equality.

492. **ida tqul elbalut aẖla metmar ennas tjib elxbar**

If you say the acorn is sweeter than the date, people will know the truth.

There are lies that nobody will accept; or, this is self-evident.

493. **ida wakalt śaba', ida drabt waja'**

If you feed them, give them their fill; if you beat them, make them feel the pain.

Half-measures are not good; when you do something, do it to its fullest.

494. **ida xellèk mul elôrs kul bla ḡsil yedeyn**

If you are allowed in a wedding party, eat without washing your hands.

Don't make plans without reckoning with possible obstacles; you have to first clear them.

495. **ida xsimek elẖakem leśkun teśki**

If you have a quarrel with the government, to whom are you going to complain?

You can't fight city hall.

496. **iîśu leklab fi rus elmajanin**

The dogs will feed on the heads of the fools.

Dumb people are always exploited by others who take advantage of their foolishness.

497. **iji men tèli wiâyet ya mèli**

He comes from behind and yells "my money."

A Johnny-come-lately who claims rights he doesn't have.

498. **imut elfar uma yeśba'ś elḡar**

The rat will die, and the hole will not be satisfied.

There is a limit to the sexual desires (or activity) of men, but not to those of women.

499. **imutu nas bsa'd nas**

Some people will die and bring luck to others.

The disaster of some is the success of others.

500. **inśala tkun exretna xir men uletna**

May our end be better than our beginning.

501. **îś belmen ya kamun ḡodwa nesqik**

Live on the dew, cumin; tomorrow I will water you.

Promises always repeated and never kept; mañana.

502. **îś nhar serduk ula âm djaja**

Live as a rooster for a day and not as a hen for a year.

What counts is not the length of life but its quality.

503. **iśuf h̲adbet ḡeyru uma iśufś h̲adbtu**

He sees his neighbor's hump but doesn't see his own.

We are quick in pointing to others' deficiencies and faults, but we are blind to our own.

504. **ixaraj âynu bèś ixaraj âyneyn sah̲bu**

He will gouge his own eye so that he can gouge both eyes of another.

One person was granted a wish on condition that another will get double. He asked for gouging out one of his eyes so that the other will lose both his eyes. This applies to wicked, envious, and hating people, and sometimes to litigious persons.

505. **izid âlik leyla izid âlik h̲ila**

One night older, one trick smarter.

Wisdom grows with age.

506. **izid leh̲tab wiqul ennar mneyn**

He adds wood and says, "What caused the fire?"

He sows the seeds of the trouble, or the conflict, and plays innocent.

507. **ja essayf uwelleyna kif kif**

The summer came and we became equal.

Poor and rich are equal in the summer because there is no need for expensive warm clothes as in winter.

508. **ja iâwen fi qbar buh ahrablu belfès**

He came to help dig his father's grave and then fled with the pick.

The person on whom we counted most proved to be the biggest problem.

509. **ja iduq sbah̲ ilaqam**

He came just to taste and he ended up eating voraciously.

Some people abuse your kindness.

510. **ja itobha a'maha**

He came to cure her, he blinded her.

By trying to remedy a situation, you make it worse. If it ain't broke, don't fix it.

511. **jarek leqrib xir men xuk lebîd**

Your close neighbor is better than your distant brother.

512. **jebt grelu iwanesni h̲al âynu xawefni**

I brought a pet for pleasure and companionship, he opened his eyes and scared me.

What could normally be a source of comfort turned out to be a source of worry.

513. **jeytek aziza ama elma'jun ufa**

You are very welcome, but the jam is finished.

Sarcastic: Sorry, you came to extract something from us, but there is nothing to give you.

514. **jmilek âl bdaya' daya'**

The care you take of perishable produce is useless.

If you do a favor for a wicked person, it is a total loss.

515. **jralu ma jra letayr elli dâlu qam nofseleyl**

The same thing happened to him that happened to the bird; the one who cursed him did it at midnight.

He is a victim of a very cruel curse. Midnight is, according to legend, the best hour for a curse to "work." He is a victim of a plot, or a bad action.

516. **jrè âliha uma lẖaqha, qal ma'tuqa fi sabil ellah**

He ran after her and could not catch her; he said: "be safe for God's sake."

When one cannot achieve a certain goal, rather than admit his defeat, he finds excuses for abandoning the pursuit.

517. **juân utaẖ fi ẖśiśa**

He is hungry and he found a plant [to eat].

When the opportunity knocks on your door, grab it.

518. **jwab ifaraẖ ula qa'da tqaraẖ**

A letter that makes you happy is better than a presence that makes you miserable.

Separation can be good if it can improve your life (like a husband or son finding a job far from home rather than be unemployed, unhappy, and living with the family).

519. **kabart belẖmar usarajtu, qam yebki ẖata berda'tu**

I respected the donkey and harnessed it; he started crying for a saddle.

When you give someone something, he asks for more.

520. **ka'keslu yerja' laslu**

Anger him, he will return to his nature.

You think he is quite cool tempered; wait until you see him when he is angry, he will show you his real self.

521. **kanet tesxer wellèt ta'mel èxtef**

She used to snore, now she spits.

Story: a man had a wife who snored heavily; he consulted an old man who advised him to pull out her front teeth, which he did. After that, not only did she continue to snore, but it worsened and was accompanied by spitting. Sometimes, by trying to fix something, you ruin it completely. If it ain't broke, don't fix it.

522. **katar âl mluk imelluk**

If you abuse, even the angels will be tired of you.

Don't abuse kindness or hospitality; you will be the loser.

523. **katar elmuna walu tkun elmra mejnuna**

Add more condiments and ingredients even if your wife is crazy [the food will be very good].

524. **katar leh̲nut wa'ti la'duk yotbox**

Add more spices, and let your enemy do the cooking.

A dish without spices is bland and tasteless. The spices make a good dish; if you add the good spices, you can even let your enemy do the cooking, and he won't be able to ruin the dish.

525. **katar men elâsèl yemsat**

Too much honey will ruin the cake.

Too much of even a good thing spoils it.

526. **kber elfellus uraba errius**

The chick grew up and now has a big head.

When somebody suddenly finds wealth or power, he becomes a braggart, proud and haughty.

527. **kber haman wetla' lessuq**

Haman grew up and went to the market.

The enemy of the Jews, Haman, is powerful; who knows what evil could come from him if he gets more power. Applies to an enemy who becomes powerful and dangerous.

528. **kbert ya fayar wa'melt bâybes**

You grew up, little mouse, and you grew a little tail.

Who do you think you are? Have you forgotten what you were before, poor and insignificant!

529. **kbirek âla matsènsu usḡirek âla matrabih**

An old person will act according to his habits, and a young person according to his education.

The stress is on the second part: education should start at a very young age, at infancy.

530. **kelb ẖay ula sayd miyet**

A living dog is better than a dead lion.

You are feared, or respected, as long as you are alive and powerful. Dead, you are worth nothing.

531. **kelb nbaẖ la âdar ula jraẖ**

A barking dog did not bite or wound anyone.

More bark than bite—just talk, no action.

532. **kelma felwej ula âśra felqfa**

A word in your face is better than ten behind your back.

Be straightforward and speak your mind openly and honestly.

533. **kelma fi waqtha ettura ẖalletha**

A word in its time, the Torah permitted it.

Don't hesitate to say things that are appropriate and timely, even if they are difficult to accept.

534. **kelmet la ma tjib bla**

The word "no" never causes problems.

When in doubt, abstain. Never promise anything which you can't keep.

535. **kelmet mèt ma fiha tbèt**

The word "dead" needs no verification.

Death is certain and irreversible.

536. **kelmet za' tsuq ejj'mal elkol**

The word "za' " leads all camels.

Same rules for everyone; we are all in the same boat.

537. **kèn felqra' wala felbeytenjal**

He was in the zucchini, and he moved to the eggplants.

This is used mainly in conversation, when someone abruptly changes subjects, or evades the issue.

538. **kèn kèri wella mul eddar**

He was a tenant and became the landlord.

Applies to a person who is arrogant, who arrogates himself the right to interfere, to command on matters which are none of his business.

539. **kènlek men leylet edxul ya mahbul**

You should have done it on the wedding night, you fool.

The story is about two brothers who got married at the same time, but one was respected and well taken care of by his wife, and the other, on the contrary, was neglected, hungry, dirty, and the laughing stock of his neighbors. One day, the latter asked the former about his secret. The happy brother responded: "On the wedding night, I bought a sharp sword and asked my servant to bring a cat in a bag and let it go free as soon as he saw my wife. The servant did as ordered. When my wife appeared, he let the cat free and I took my sword and cut the cat in halves. That made my wife fear and respect me, because she imagined what would befall her if she neglected her duties. This is, my dear brother, all my secret." Upon hearing that, the neglected brother went to buy a sword and ordered his servant to do the same thing. But when he raised his arm to cut the cat, his wife of some years exclaimed, "You should have done it on the wedding night, you fool."

540. **kèn qaêd bès elh̲ayt**

For no reason, he got up and kissed the wall.

He asked for trouble.

541. **kif elâqrab fi âdilet jrad**

Like a scorpion in a basket of grasshoppers.

Something incongruous; or, one strong individual can be beaten by a group of weaker ones. Strength is in numbers.

542. **kif elẖuta motliya bessabun**

Like a fish covered with soap.

Very slippery; you can't hold it in your hands. For persons: a two-faced hypocrite.

543. **kif elẖut ida xrej melma imut**

Like the fish, if it goes out of water, it dies.

A person who moves to another city, or takes another job for which he has no experience, is very unhappy.

544. **kif elkarmus fi âdila**

Like figs in a basket.

Wrinkled like a fig left to dry in a wicker basket; or, insignificant like a small fig in a huge basket.

545. **kif elmelẖ ma iḡib âla tbix**

Like salt, it is in all dishes.

He is never absent from any event, is always there.

546. **kif elqatus inik wisiẖ**

Like the cat, yelling while enjoying sex.

He complains even when he should be happy.

547. **kif elxanfusa la tettakel la yelâbu biha**

Like the roach, you can't eat it and you can't play with it.

It (or he) is worth nothing.

548. **kif elyebra teksi ennas uhiya ôriana**

Like the needle, it gets people dressed but it is bare.

Someone helping others and forgetting himself.

549. **kif erriya ertaba uqalet edhan**

Like the lung, soft but without fat.

The lungs are soft and attractive (to eat), but there is no fat (nourishing!) in them.

He speaks softly but that's all: no action, no help from him. A hypocrite.

550. **kif eśśamâ tdawi ânnas uta<u>h</u>raq nefsha**

Like the candle, it gives light to others and burns itself.

Someone sacrificing himself for the benefit of others.

551. **kif leqfel âla uden ejjarra**

[It is] like a lock on the pitcher's ears.

This lock is useless; anybody can pull it and break the pitcher's ears.

552. **kif mosmar ju<u>h</u>a**

Like Juha's nail.

Story: Juha, the comic figure in Tunisian folklore, agreed to sell his house on the condition that he leave a nail in the bedroom wall. The buyer agreed to this trivial term. After he sold the house, Juha claimed his right to visit his "property" (the nail) every day. The nail of Juha denotes a nuisance, a loose end, unfinished business.

553. **kif mul erriśa, qayemha nadem, <u>h</u>atetha nadem**

Like the owner of the feather: damn if he takes it, damn if he doesn't.

Story: A man found a jewel shaped like a feather. He bent to pick it up and found inscribed on it: "You will regret if you take it, and you will regret if you don't take it."

554. **kif sara<u>h</u> xaltu**

Like the shepherd working for his aunt.

Story: A shepherd took his aunt's cattle to graze. He thought his aunt would make him rich and she thought her nephew would not charge for his services. Hence the big fight.

The terms of any deal should be spelled out very clearly in advance.

555. **kif serwal elâskri men zok elzok**

Like the trousers of the soldiers, from buttocks to buttocks.

Someone (or something) that is always moving around, not stable.

556. **kif xuh la iâyruh**

Like his brother, nobody will mock him.

He is of the same breed, dumb like the whole family.

557. **klèm elâdu idah̲ak; klèm essah̲eb ibèki**

The words of the enemy make you laugh; the words of the friend make you cry.

Unpleasant reproaches coming from your enemy are expected and not respected; from your friend, they are true and sincere; you value them, and repent.

558. **klèm elleyl medhun bezzebda, waqtli yesbah̲ esbah̲ idub**

The words of the night are covered with butter; in the morning, they melt away.

Women should not believe the promises of men made at night in bed, because their only purpose is to satisfy their sexual desires; the next day they are forgotten.

559. **klèw tâmna wensèw esmna**

They ate our food, and forgot our names.

Ingratitude: not to be thankful for a favor, not to send a note of thanks for a service rendered.

560. **kleyma fessbah̲ ukleyma felâśiya trod lemselma ihudiya**

One word in the morning and one in the evening make the Moslem woman become Jewish.

By repeating, you can influence the mind and decisions of a person; propaganda and indoctrination are very powerful tools.

561. **kob lebrayma âla fomha, kol bnaya tetla' lomha**

As the cover fits the pot, a daughter fits her mother.

A daughter looks and behaves like her mother.

562. **kol âtla fiha xeyr**

All obstacles have their blessings.

Close to: "Every cloud has a silver lining." Don't worry or get angered if something does not work as you plan; you may be lucky. Example: if you miss a flight and the plane you missed crashes later.

563. **kol ful lèhi fi nawaru**

Every kind of fava is busy with its own flower.

Each one minds his own business; don't interfere.

564. **kol h̲arka fiha barka**

Every activity has its blessing.

Don't sit idle.

565. **kol lah̲ma fiha âdma**

Every piece of meat has a bone.

No roses without thorns.

566. **kol mah̲qur ând rabi maśkur**

All despised people are praised by God.

567. **kol nar ttayeb âśatha**

Each fire cooks its own dinner.

Everyone knows what is good for him and how to solve his

own problems; or, each one feels his own pain and nobody else's.

568. **kol qard fi âyn omu ġzal**

A monkey, in the eyes of his mother, is a gazelle.

Motherly love blinds the mother who does not see her children's defects.

569. **kol saâ uôlmha**

Each hour and its knowledge.

At different times, different customs; things change, nothing stays the same.

570. **kol sayd fi ḡabtu gatal**

Any lion is a killer in his own forest.

Everyone is master in his own territory; or, one knows and understands best in his own field of specialization.

571. **kol śey deyn ẖata ndib elxodeyn**

Everything is a debt, even the scratching of cheeks [when mourning a dead person].

572. **kol śey men mratu ẖata rbat sabatu**

Everything is from his wife, even tying his shoelaces.

All the burden is on the women, even the smallest chores that are personal; or, the success or failure of a man depends on his wife; she can make him rich, and she can also ruin him.

573. **kol śey nsib ẖata lulad wensib**

Everything is luck, even the children and the son-in-law.

574. **kol skafi ẖafi**

All shoemakers barefoot.

People who take care of others and forget themselves.

575. **kol wah̲ed âqlu fi rasu ya'ref xlasu**

Everyone knows what is good for him.

Nobody will learn from other people's mistakes; no use interfering in other people's problems.

576. **kol wah̲ed ikeyel âla saû**

Each one will buy [grain] according to his measuring cup.

Don't live beyond your means; spend according to your income; or, everyone knows how to take care of himself.

577. **kol wah̲ed ya'ref weyn yedfen buh**

Everyone knows where to bury his father.

Don't interfere in domestic matters; everyone knows what is good for him.

578. **kol wah̲ed yendeb âla grih̲tu**

Each one will mourn his own loss.

No one will suffer for others.

579. **kont fi dar elmellès welleyt fi dar ennajar**

I was in the house of the plasterer; I found myself in the house of the carpenter.

The situation has changed; or, he changed the subject.

580. **kotrot ennowm twerret elkesl welkesl iwerret elfqar**

Too much sleep brings laziness, and laziness brings poverty.

581. **kotrtu mśuma uqaltu h̲arfa**

Too much of it is bad, and too little of it is bad.

Everything should be done (or taken) in moderation.

582. **kul bśahwtek welbes bśahwet ḡeyrek**

Eat according to your desires, but dress according to the desires of others.

While eating is a private and discreet matter, dressing is for showing off and must conform to the rules of fashion.

583. **kul korh, elbes korh, ula zwaj elkorh**

Eat what you hate, wear the clothes you hate, but never marry what you hate.

584. **kul mâ elwakal wexdem mâ elxadam**

Eat with the gourmet [good eater] and work with the diligent worker.

Rub elbows with those who know and understand what they are doing.

585. **kul ma trod, ejjbal tethed**

Eat without refilling, the mountains will be destroyed.

One cannot spend when he is not producing income, otherwise he will become destitute.

586. **kul uwekkel**

Eat and feed others.

Don't be selfish. Look after your own interest but don't forget the others. Live and let live!

587. **kuna sh̲ab welflus raduna êdwan**

We were friends, and the money made us enemies.

Keep money (loans, partnerships, etc.) out of friendship; otherwise, it will destroy it.

588. **kun dayf umuś klufi**

Be a guest and not nosy.

Do not get involved, do not interfere, in things which are none of your business, especially when you are a guest.

589. **kun sayd ukulni**

Be a lion, and eat me.

Behave as a man, not a coward; tell the truth, don't hide anything, even if it is detrimental to me.

590. **la deyn ula dâ elwaldeyn**

No debt and no parents' curse.

Avoid debts, do with less but pay cash.

591. **la ẖbib ella ẖbib eśedda ama ferxa ennas elkol ẖbab**

The real friend is a friend when we are in distress, but in abundance, all are friends.

A friend in need is a friend indeed.

592. **la îd la thur qamet elqẖab tzur**

It is no holiday, and the whores went visiting.

Something unusual happened, what is the surprise?

593. **la iẖotna fi fom xalq la belbatel la belẖaq**

May we not be in the mouth of the people, whether true or not.

It is better not to become a subject of gossip.

594. **la ijo' eddib wala yebki erraî**

The wolf will not be hungry, and the shepherd will not cry.

Reach a compromise, everybody is satisfied, no one is hurt.

595. **la imut ula ixelli ennûś yetekraw**

He does not die, and he doesn't allow us to rent the coffins.

Not only doesn't he do anything, but he doesn't let anyone else do anything.

596. **la iwasax Mecca**

God forbid, let us not defile Holy Mecca.

Sarcastic: you think you are better than the rest of us, and our company may tarnish your reputation.

597. **la men fomu la men komu la melqahba elli jabet omu**

Neither his physical appearance, nor his talk, nor the whore who gave birth to his mother [are good].

When you find nothing good in a person.

598. **la men qorstek ula men âsltek**

Not your pinching, and not your honey.

I don't want anything from you, neither good nor bad.

599. **la nhabek ula nesbar âlik**

I don't love you and I can't be without you.

Damned if you do, damned if you don't

600. **la'rusa twila ubab eddar qsir**

The bride is tall, and the door opening is short.

This is said about a problem which appears to be insoluble but which can be easily resolved: the bride has only to bend a little to get through the door. The story relates how the town council was called to resolve the situation, and was divided into two "schools of thought": those who advised cutting off the bride's head so that she could pass through the door, and those who suggested cutting off her feet.

601. **la'sida rotba wellitim âlaf**

The pudding is soft and the kid is a very good eater.

The circumstances are perfect, everything fits, the result is clear.

602. **la ta'ti men yeddek ula tendem âla mè fet**

Do not give what you have in your hand, so that you do not regret what is done.

Make sure you understand all the terms of a deal before you give something which you can't get back.

603. **la tayr men itir ula fères men isir**

No bird flying, and no horse running.

It is like a desert, silent, dead.

604. **la tbèt mâlmi ula nesbah̲ sanêk**

You will not go to bed as my master, and I will not wake up as your servant.

Let us put an end to our relationship, each one for himself.

605. **la tdèxèl yeddek felmḡaḡer ula yelâsuk la'qareb**

Don't put your hand in caves, or the scorpions will sting you.

Don't venture into the unknown, you may be hurt; don't interfere in a quarrel, you will get the blame.

606. **la tesra' ula tendem âla mè fet**

Don't rush and don't regret what you have done.

607. **la thaman elxeyl ida ḡabu ula leqh̲ab ida tèbu**

Don't trust the horses if they run away, or the whores if they repent.

Once a horse has run away, he will not come back; the whore who repents will return to her previous activities. This is applied to someone whom you cannot trust.

608. **la todmon dmana bèt felhana**

Don't vouch for someone [or cosign a loan]; you will sleep in tranquility.

Because if the borrower does not pay, they will go after your property.

609. **la todmon dmana, toxrej enti noqôd ana**

Do not cosign a loan for someone else; he will go free and you will get caught.

610. **la yetxaba la leh̲bal la lehbal**

Pregnancy and madness cannot be hidden.

It is foolish to try to hide the obvious.

611. **lbes elmajen uxaraj yeddeyh melẖlaqem**

He wore the cistern and put his hands out through the pipes.

He became very angry and frightening, and dangerous.

612. **leẖmel âjmaâ riś**

The burden on a group is like feathers.

If everyone pulls his weight, the work is easy.

613. **lemra elli ma ta'refś tnawaẖ xsaret mot rajelha**

The woman who can't whine in mourning, it's a pity that her husband dies.

It is a waste to have something which you can't use, or don't know how to enjoy (i.e. money you can't spend, a huge house without children or guests, etc.).

614. **lèśkun tẖarqas ya mart la'ma**

For whom you are wearing makeup, you, wife of the blind!

Unnecessary and useless action.

615. **letrab ula lulad leqẖab**

To the dust and not to the sons of bitches.

I prefer to throw it away (money, food, etc.) rather than give it to wicked and unworthy people.

616. **leyla felfarś leyla fenna'ś**

One night in bed, the next in the grave.

We never know when we will die; life is short and unpredictable. We must enjoy it the best we can; or, we must do good on this earth.

617. **litim lqa wesla bka ẖata a'ma êyneh**

The orphan found an excuse, he cried until he became blind.

Someone who needed only the slightest pretext to act is

given it and uses it as an excuse for his action. Examples: a boss wants to fire his employee, and the employee comes late to work; or, a dictator wants to attack his neighbor and the latter inadvertently crosses the border.

618. **lma mqabelna welâtaś qatelna**

Water is in front of us and thirst is killing us.

We have something very important, vital, and we can't use it.

619. **loqma men dari ula xobza men jari**

A mouthful from my house is better than a whole loaf from my neighbor.

Do with less and don't take from others.

620. **lqa xatem âla qad sobû**

He found a ring that fits his finger.

He found something, or someone, that is exactly what he wanted, a perfect fit, or a perfect match, a very compatible wife or friend.

621. **lsènek sawanek, sontu sanek, xontu xanek**

Your tongue is your rock; take care of it, it will take care of you; betray it, it will betray you.

Beware of what you say.

622. **lsèn ezzeyn yedfa' fedeyn**

A beautiful tongue pays your debt.

If you speak nicely and show respect to your debtor, he will be more understanding of your difficulties and more patient; it is as if you paid him back.

623. **lukèn eddeyf iji belkrara mul eddar âlih belxsara**

Even if the guest comes loaded with gifts, the host is always the loser.

624. **lukèn ejmel ifiq b<u>h</u>adbtu iti<u>h</u> uteqta' raqbtu**

If the camel could notice his hump, he would fall and break his neck.

Lucky are those who are not aware of their defects.

625. **lukèn elâdma fiha wedneyn iqimuha tneyn**

If the egg had handles, it would be lifted by two people.

When you share a burden, it becomes much easier.

626. **lukèn elbuma fiha xeyr ma ixalfuha esayada**

If the owl had anything good at all, the hunters would not let it live.

One usually does not refuse anything; if he does, that means the offer is not good at all.

627. **lukèn elkedb <u>h</u>oja essodq enja wenja**

If lying can provide an excuse, telling the truth is much better.

628. **lukèn elxox idèwi kèn idèwi nefsu men eddud**

If the peaches could cure you, they would cure themselves of the worms.

Don't ask advice from someone who has the same problems as yours and can't resolve them.

629. **lukèn eśśerka fiha xeyr yetśarku tneyn fi mra**

If there is any profit in partnership, two will share a woman.

630. **lukèn jufi gzaza nemlaha bxobza udjaja; lukèn jufi damus nemlaha belxanfus**

If my belly is of glass, I will fill it with bread and chicken; if it is a closed cellar, I will fill it with cockroaches.

One should always appear content and satisfied in public and keep one's problems to oneself.

631. **lukèn muś a'dam erras nodxol men âyn elyebra**

[Says the mouse:] If it were not for the bones in my head, I would pass through the eye of the needle.

This proverb applies to someone who gets by easily and adapts to all situations.

632. **lukèn mús la'nad matoẖbol ennsa**

If not for imitation, women would not get pregnant.

Most things people do are imitations of their family, friends, and neighbors, in order not to be different.

633. **lukèn muś melẖawja ma nrodok rajel**

If not because of the need, I would never make you a man.

A widow in need will make a man out of her ten-year-old son.

When one is in need, one makes do with anything.

634. **lukèn muś nakol xobzti unetma' ferbaya' mtaêk ma nśarkek**

If I can't eat my whole loaf of bread and a quarter of yours, I will not be your partner.

Partnership is not good.

635. **lukèn muś omi fennsa tji fihom elkansa**

If not for my mother, let the plague take all women.

A misogynistic attitude of someone who has suffered at the hands of his wife.

636. **lukèn omi ẖabetni mella'deyma radetni**

If my mother had loved me, she would have made me return the egg.

Based on a story of a young boy: he stole an egg the first time and brought it to his mother who congratulated him for his deed; then he stole chickens, sheep, and cows, and was finally caught and put in jail. He accused his mother of not having punished him on his first theft. The moral is clear: never start a bad thing like stealing, lying, cheating, drinking, or using drugs. And for parents: punish your child the first time he does something wrong.

637. **lukèn s͟hat endbi, lukèn sabet endbi**

If it does not rain, cry; if it rains, cry.

Story: a mother had two daughters, one in the north and one in the south. One is happy when it rains and the other is unhappy when it rains. The mother is always unhappy because one of her daughters is always unhappy.

Applies to a situation where you're "damned if you do, damned if you don't."

638. **lukèn xu yenfa' xu ma yebki h͟ad àla buh**

If a brother could care for his brother, nobody would cry at the loss of his father.

Brotherly love will never match fatherly love.

639. **luwa luwa maklet ejjirèn h͟luwa**

The cooking of the neighbors is sweet.

You don't appreciate what you have, and envy what other people have; the grass is greener on the other side.

640. **ma a'ma kèn a'ma elqalb**

There is no blindness but the blindness of the heart.

641. **ma àndu bès̓ ixalas elh͟afaf westaden eddiaf**

He doesn't have any money to pay the barber, and he invited guests.

One should avoid superfluous spending when one can't provide for the necessities.

642. **ma bars̓ ellek ibur ezza'fran!**

If the bad spice could sell, certainly the saffron will.

If ugly girls get married, the beautiful ones certainly will.

643. **ma bqalek kèn fi lown elmalf**

The only thing left to worry about is the color of the garment.

You don't have money to buy a suit and you worry about details like the color of the suit.

644. **mada melmethumin felh̲abs**

Many innocent people are in jail.

When an innocent person is accused of something he didn't do.

645. **madwar kelb uba'busu âla bara**

A dog's niche, and his tail outside.

This house is very small; even a dog couldn't fit in, as his tail will be dangling outside.

646. **maḡzen maḡluq ula kerya mśuma**

A closed store is better than a bad rental [tenant].

Don't be tempted by some offer; be patient, investigate, and make sure it is O.K. before you commit yourself to anything.

647. **mahbul men qal lulad felkobr yexdmu âliya**

Crazy is the one who says, "When I am old, the children will support me."

648. **mahbul men śwa âdma umahbul men tma' fiha**

Crazy is the one who grilled an egg and crazy is the one who was tempted to eat it.

A foolish action followed by a more foolish one.

649. **ma ibur h̲mel fizqaq, ida ma iqimuh emmalih iqimuh essorraq**

A package will never be left unwanted in the street. If it is not taken by its owner, it will be taken by thieves.

650. **ma ihèd errtal kèn erratleyn**

The only thing that can destroy one pound is two pounds.

If you oppress weaker people, the stronger will oppress you.

651. **ma ih̲ès ejamra kan elli ya'fes âliha**

Only the person who walks on embers feels the fire.

No one can feel the pain, suffering, or agony of someone else.

652. **ma ijib elfsad kan elksad**

Idleness brings vice.

653. **ma iji elful kan lelli maâńduś ezrus**

The [hard] fava beans come only to those who have no teeth [to break the beans before eating].

He can't enjoy what he has; or, he does not deserve what he has (money, job, house, wife, children) because he does not know how to enjoy the possession or the relationship.

654. **ma imut h̲ad mkamaś**

No one dies wrinkled. [When a person dies, they stretch his limbs and his body.]

In the end, all are the same. Death is the great equalizer.

655. **ma iquluś qadaś g̅ab, iqulu èś jab**

They don't say "how long has he been away"; they say "what did he bring."

People are selfish and greedy.

656. **ma iśed bir kèn somâ**

Only a tower can fill a well.

If you want to fight a person, or make war on another country, you should oppose the same strength, or intelligence.

657. **ma lqaś xobza ilemha lqa árusa ikalamha**

He did not find a loaf of bread to take; he found a bride to talk to.

He is confused in his priorities.

658. **ma mètś qatluh la'rab**

He didn't die, he was killed by the bedouins.

What is the difference? It is exactly the same thing.

659. **ma nah̲ essers lama xlat elh̲mada**

The town of Sers could live in peace only after the town of Hamada had been destroyed.

As long as your enemy is alive, you will have to worry; or, help arrived too late, after all was lost.

660. **ma naqes elma âl faqus kèn tah̲rik ezrus**

The only difference between the cucumber and water is the moving of the teeth.

Things appear to be different, but in essence they are the same.

661. **ma naqes elmaśnuq kèn maklet elh̲alwa**

The only thing a hanged man needs is a piece of candy.

First things first: save your life before you think about the luxury of eating candy.

662. **ma nhamnek ya ben elqaran walu yenbet âla dahrek elh̲śiś**

I will not trust you, son of a bitch, even if grass grows on your back.

Story: a sailor's boat was one day capsized by a whale; some time later, while sailing, the sailor saw a small island covered with grass. He steered his boat away, thinking it was another whale camouflaged with grass to deceive him. Moral: you cheated me once, I don't trust you any more, even if you wear a disguise or pretend to be nice.

663. **mard elqola âla h̲jar elbir**

The illness of the jug on the stone of the well.

Something fake, an excuse (for the jug is happy to be filled).

664. **marhun fettah̲fifa jayeb eśhud temlek**

He still owes money for the ceremony of the haircut [before a wedding], and he brought the notaries.

He puts the cart before the horse.

665. **maśaya ujaraya uma takolś eśśîr**

She walks, she runs, and she does not eat barley [talking about a donkey].

Somebody who is exploited by his boss, or his friends. They want him to do all the work with no compensation.

666. **ma śemtet fiya kèn botni usenneya**

I must submit to two things only: my belly and my teeth.

When something horrible happens (like a death in the family), you may decide not to talk, not to wash .... But you must eat (belly) and sometimes you can't help laughing (teeth).

667. **ma tamaś doxan bla nar**

There is no smoke without fire.

668. **matamaś qatus yestad elrabi**

There is no cat that hunts for God's sake.

No one does anything if it is not in his interest.

669. **matamaś śojra ma kabha errih̲; ida ma kabha habha**

There is no tree that is not brought down by the wind; if not brought down, at least bent.

Everybody has his faults, makes mistakes, and at times fails. Nobody is perfect.

670. **ma ta'meliś melẖaba qoba**

Don't make a dome out of a grain.

Don't make a mountain out of a molehill.

671. **ma tâned lebẖar ida ẖmaq werkik ida ându lẖaq**

Do not argue with the ocean if it is angry and with the nerd if he is right.

672. **ma ta'ref bkar omok ẖata tjik mart buk**

You can value your mother only after your stepmother comes.

Don't take things for granted; their replacement could be very bad. Appreciate what you have.

673. **ma ta'ref ẖad ẖata tjawru**

You don't know a person until you have been his neighbor.

By being close to someone for some time, you are bound to know him well; the appearance is misleading.

674. **ma ta'ref waẖed lama tnasbu ula tjawru**

You really know a man only after he has been your son-in-law or your neighbor.

675. **ma taxod kalam essukara fi ma iqulu**

Do not believe the words of the drunk.

When they are sober, they will not remember what they said.

676. **ma tâzi kan elli xrej men blèdu umatet om uladu wetẖawej luladu**

Have pity only on someone who has left his hometown, who lost the mother of his children, and who became a burden on his children.

677. **ma tbaza' mè lama tujed mè**

Don't spill water before you find water.

Hold on to what you have until you find better.

678. **ma tdèxèl eldarek kèn elqamh̲ wešîr, ama elh̲oms igarba'**

Let into your house only wheat and barley, but the chick-peas will roll all over.

You must be very selective in choosing your guests. The good ones, like the wheat and the barley, will stay in place, but the bad ones, like the chickpeas, will roll all over the place, see what they shouldn't see and sometimes cause damage.

679. **ma tebki kèn âla maḡzen xali**

Cry only over a deserted store.

Applies to a store without customers, or to a house without children.

680. **ma teh̲mar elèyneyn kèn âl waldeyn**

The eyes become red only for the parents.

When parents are insulted, their children get angry (red eyes), and fight for their honor.

681. **ma tekber elâyn âla elh̲ajeb**

The eye should not feel superior to the eyebrow.

One should never feel superior to his parents; they are part of him and they also protect him.

682. **ma tḡati èyn eššems belḡorbal**

Don't cover the sun's eye with a sieve.

Don't hide things which are conspicuous, don't deny what is evident.

683. **ma thaman bedkayar walu ikun qad leffayar**

Don't trust the male even if he is as small as a mouse.

If you are a female, avoid the company of males even if they appear sexually innocent.

684. **ma t<u>h</u>el essedqa lama yeśbû mali eddar**

Charity is allowed only after the family is satisfied.

Charity begins at home.

685. **ma tjawarś tlibek uma tsèkènś ba<u>h</u>dak nsibek**

Don't have your creditor as your neighbor and don't let your son-in-law live with you.

686. **ma to<u>h</u>sob bagrek kèn ba'd ettebiba**

Count your cattle only after the plague.

Don't count your chickens before they are hatched.

687. **ma toxroj elôbra kèn fi diar elkobra**

Dishonor destroys only great families.

688. **ma tqos yed essaraq qbel ma yesraq**

Don't cut the thief's hand before he steals.

Do not prejudge others; give them a chance, you may be mistaken in your suspicions.

689. **ma tqulś elma âlaś jrè**

Don't tell on what the water was flowing.

Story: two accomplices killed a man and threw the corpse into the river. Water flowed over his blood. They promised each other not to say one word about their act, not even about the water. Hence the meaning: let us keep it top secret, and not say anything, not even the slightest thing connected with our secret.

690. **ma tsakar bab <u>h</u>ata tefta<u>h</u> bab axor**

Don't shut a door until you open another one.

Don't throw away what you have in hand, a job for example, before you are sure to find something better.

691. **ma ttarad elkelb lama ta'ref śkun mulah**

Don't chase out the dog without knowing who his master is.

Don't start trouble with someone without knowing his strength or his supporters. Don't undertake any endeavor without studying the consequences.

692. **ma twasi itim âla nwaẖ**

Don't teach an orphan how to mourn and whine.

Don't give advice to experts.

693. **ma uẖtab ulsèn artab**

Water and wood and a soft tongue.

What is the coffee you buy in a coffee shop? Water, wood to boil it, and nice talk. And for that, they charge you a lot of money! Or: when you pay much more for the service than for the thing itself.

694. **mâwej elkerêyn ma qamś bemra iqum betneyn?**

The bow-legged man, if he did not support one wife, could he support two?

A good-for-nothing man.

695. **ma xowfiś âla mardu xowfi âla xiban tabû**

I am not worrying about his disease, I am worrying about the spoiling of his character.

In education, a good character is more important than physical health.

696. **ma yahdru leqlal kèn men fom lexwabi**

The small jugs speak only from the mouth of the big jars.

Children repeat what they hear at home.

697. **ma ya'ref saraq kèn saraq**

Only a thief knows a thief.

Birds of a feather flock together.

698. **ma ya'refś elqantra men wadha**

He cannot tell the bridge from the river.

He is dumb; he does not understand anything.

699. **ma ya'ref xra lama iduqu**

He recognizes the excrement only after he tastes it.

He does not trust other people; he does not learn from their experiences.

700. **ma yebki ettayr melxeyr**

The bird will not cry when you are good to him.

Everybody is happy when they receive gifts and when people are nice to them.

701. **ma yekber fi jedru kan leqra'**

Only the pumpkin grows bigger than its root.

Human beings should not feel themselves to be superior to their origins (parents).

702. **ma yekber ras kèn ma iśib ras**

One head will grow only after another head becomes old.

It is very difficult to raise children; it takes the whole life of the parents.

703. **ma yetla' lbuh ulomu kèn elfakrun**

Only the tortoise resembles its father and mother.

This applies to a situation where the parents are disappointed in their child who does not resemble them, sometimes physically, but especially in attitude and moral conduct.

704. **ma yetxaltu lama yetśabbu**

Only those who resemble each other become friends.

Birds of a feather flock together.

705. **mejnuna uzaḡrtulha fi wedneyha**

She is crazy and they yelled in her ear.

From bad to worse.

706. **mèklet elbènèy fi dar lihud**

The meal of the mason in the house of the Jews [a very good meal, rich and varied].

Something very expensive; it costs and arm and a leg.

707. **mèklet essyuda ula tferfiś edyab**

The eating of the lions is better than the tearing of the wolves.

It is better to be eaten up by a lion than to be torn to pieces by wolves. A clean job, even if detrimental, is better than a messy one.

708. **mella triẖa klatha jebti lukèn muś jeyt ana fiha**

My coat got a good beating; the only problem is that I was in it.

I wouldn't care what happens to the world if I were not part of it.

709. **melwarda toxrej śoka umeśśoka toxrej warda**

From the rose comes a thorn, and from the thorn comes a rose.

A good child may come from bad parents, and vice versa.

710. **men baysa leqraysa ẖata weslu el sidi ben îsa**

From a kiss to a pinch until they arrived in Sidi Ben Îsa.

A boy and a girl had better not start any flirtation, because this will lead to the "holy" parts (Sidi Ben Îsa is a saint).

711. **men beyt elbeyt yetzad xeyt; men dar eldar yetzad sonar**

From room to room, a thread is added; from house to house, a stone is added.

Gossip distorts the message and exaggerates the news.

712. **men h̲asek ya bufseya beyn luraq bèyet**

Who will notice you, little bird, sleeping among the leaves.

You are insignificant.

713. **men nafqtu tbèn âśah**

From his spending [on food] you will guess his dinner.

His external appearance will shed light on his real personality.

714. **men soḡru yetâwej elfaqus**

The cucumber gets crooked from its "infancy."

A certain kind of cucumber grows crooked, not straight, from the very beginning. Education should start early in life.

715. **men somâ lqa' bir**

From the top of a tower to the bottom of a well.

What a difference? There is no comparison. Or: he fell in disgrace, and lost everything.

716. **men tronja lefranja uqbar lihud**

From Tronja to Fronja and the Jewish cemetery.

He has been everywhere, he has seen everything.

717. **men zbiba yesker**

He gets drunk from a raisin.

It is not difficult to confuse him. The slightest thing makes him mad; he is unpredictable.

718. **mèśi betwali kif bowlet ejjmel**

He is going backward like the camel's urination.

He is going from bad to worse, regressing all the time.

719. **mèt ejmel wetfarqu la'dayel**

The camel is dead and the sacks are separated.

When the father dies, the children separate.

720. **mh̲abti fik ya romdan h̲ata nsum âwaśrek**

How much I love you, O Ramadan [Moslem month of fasting] that I should fast the extra days.

I do only what is absolutely necessary, and even that, reluctantly. Don't ask me to do more.

721. **mim msakra mneyn dxalha labyad**

The letter Mim ["m"] is a closed circle; from where could the white [inside of the circle] enter into it?

He is dumb; don't expect an intelligent word from him.

722. **mneyn dxallek elêyn ya mâwjet elkerêyn**

How could the evil eye hit you, you, the bow-legged one!

Nobody will envy someone who has no qualities, only defects.

723. **mneyn hak la'rayef, men hak eśśojra**

Where is this branch from? From that tree.

Like father, like son.

724. **mneyn tdawarha telqaha ka'ka**

However you turn it, a circle is always a circle.

There is no solution to this problem.

725. **mo'rfet errjal knuz**

Good connections are treasures.

726. **mot ennas ând ennas kif elli raqed benâs**

The death of a person you don't know is as if he were asleep.

Only the aggrieved person can feel the pain.

727. **mqadam felharb mwaxar ferrateb**

First in combat, last in reward.

728. **mśa lejama' lqah mag̅luq qalu jèt mennek muś menni**

He went to the place of prayer and found it closed; he said: it came from you, not from me.

When you prepare to do something reluctantly and, by chance, something happens that makes it unnecessary and frees you from the chore, you are happy.

729. **mśa yotrod rawah âsar**

He [a bull] went to impregnate a cow, and he came back a fetus.

His mission failed completely.

730. **mta' ellben feśśan umta' elma felma**

What came from the milk is in the purse and what came from the water is in the water.

Story: a pilgrim, on his way to Mecca, stopped for some rest on the bank of the Nile River. He pulled his purse and began counting the pieces of silver that remained for the trip. Suddenly, an eagle plunged and took the money in his talons; he dropped part in the Nile and part in the pilgrim's purse. To the surprise of his companions, the man said that he was a milkman and he used to add water to the milk. The eagle dropped the money of the water in the Nile so that he could reach Mecca, purified of his sins.

Everyone will pay for his bad actions, sooner or later. Crime doesn't pay.

731. **muhal bèś idum hal**

No situation is eternal.

Everything changes, all is relative, patience is the best remedy for everything.

732. **mul ettaj yehtaj**

The crowned will [also] be in need.

Even the king needs someone or something.

733. **muś honi mul elh̲anut**

The shopkeeper is not here.

When you talk to someone who does not pay attention to what you say; he is absent-minded, or confused.

734. **muś kif weldha kif rbibha**

Her stepson is not like her son.

You can't love an adopted child like your own.

735. **muś kol abyad śah̲ma umuś kol akh̲al fah̲ma**

Not all white is fat [good!], and not all black is coal [bad!].

Don't rely on appearances. They may be rich with houses and jewels—but they are not happy; and vice versa.

736. **muś kol mdawar ka'k umuś kol mnaqab zlabia**

Not everything round is a kaâk, and not everything with holes is zlabia [kaâk and zlabia are pastries].

Don't rely on appearances.

737. **myeṭ daqa ula eslam âleykom**

One hundred knocks on the door are better than "good morning."

Always keep your door shut. That way, you can know your guests in advance and not be surprised by an unwelcome visitor or get caught unaware and unprepared.

738. **myet far fi ḡar ula zuj bnat fi dar**

One hundred mice in a hole are better than two daughters in a house.

Daughters should be married at a young age, and if only two of them are unmarried and living with their parents, that's hell.

739. **myet ḡorza ma ijibu xobza**

One hundred stitches cannot bring a loaf of bread.

Manual labor (as opposed to white-collar work) is not enough to make a living.

740. **myet ẖbib ula âdu waẖed**

One hundred friends are better than one enemy.

741. **myet ẖjar ula jar**

One hundred stones are better than one neighbor.

Better be stoned than have a (bad) neighbor.

742. **myet sḡar ula djaja belmonqar**

One hundred children are better than a beaked hen.

Because the hen picks at everything and ruins everything.

743. **myet xamar ula qamar**

One hundred alcoholics are better than one gambler.

744. **naḡlqu babna unoqrdu fiẖbabna**

We close our door and we criticize our friends.

Gossip is a common practice, and no one can avoid it.

745. **nas bennas unas brabi**

Some people rely on others, and some people rely on God.

Better rely on God than on man.

746. **nawala melklex ula mul eddar âliya yestenfex**

Better live in my own hut than in a house that belongs to others who despise me.

Better own a poor home than rent a rich house.

747. **nèẖi leẖyè wa'mel ma trid**

Do anything you want as long as there is no shame in it.

748. **nèẖi leqẖob wessarqa uâyer belli yebqa**

Insult a person with anything except prostitution and theft.

These two are the only things to be ashamed of; everything else is of no importance.

749. **neśki lelqadi welqadi mennu**

I complain to the judge, and the judge is involved in it [crime, injustice, bribery].

You can't fight city hall.

750. **nfakrek ya xdima bẖaltek leqdima walu telbes medheb srima**

I will remind you, maid, of your last position, even if you cover yourself with gold.

A maid who becomes rich (a nouveau riche*) should not brag when there are still people who know of her past condition.*

751. **nẖabek ya âyni ama ẖajbi a'la wa'la**

I love you, my eye, but I love my eyebrow even more.

One may love his nephews, but he loves his children even more. There are degrees in love.

752. **niyet la'ma taẖet fi ôkazu**

The bad intentions of the blind man fell into his cane.

One is punished for one's evil intentions.

753. **noqta dem ula myet saẖeb**

A drop of blood is better than one hundred friends.

Blood is thicker than water. Family is better than friendship.

754. **nośrob kèsi unorqod mâ nèsi uma iquluś sèsia bent sèsi**

I drink my cup and sleep with my people, and they will not say "beggar, daughter of beggar."

I prefer to drink poison and die rather than beg for help.

755. **ntunet elẖut men rasu**

The fish stinks from its head.

The leaders are responsible because they are corrupt; their followers only imitate them.

756. **nuẖu nuẖu kol waẖed yebki âla ruẖu**

You are all whining, but each one is whining for himself.

Although people appear to be acting together for the public welfare, in fact everyone is doing that in his own interest.

757. **obôd men eddem ula iśewhek**

Keep away from the blood, or it will soil you.

Avoid marrying in the family; that will create problems.

758. **ôd elḡala ya za'rur**

Count the fruit, wild berries.

The wild berries are very small and cheap; they can't be sold by the unit or be counted; even in great numbers, they are worthless.

Quantity but no quality.

759. **oẖna îd uxobz smid?**

Do you think we are a holiday and semolina bread?

You are always complaining about your problems as if we had none. We are not better than you, our life is not a holiday, and the bread we eat is not made of pure and refined semolina. Everybody has his share of sorrow.

760. **oẖna nâytu ya ẖbabna uhuma iâytu ya klabna**

We call them "our friends" and they call us "our dogs."

Love not reciprocated; good deeds and bad retribution.

761. **om âśra tmut taẖt ẖajra**

The mother of ten will die under a stone.

Ten children cannot take care of their mother, while she is able to raise all of them.

762. **omi xir men xalti womi tśuf fard âyn**

My mother looks better than my aunt, and my mother is one-eyed.

For a bad situation, there is worse.

763. **oqtlu yesbaẖ ẖay**

Kill him [at night], he will be alive in the morning.

764. **ôrian ezzok fi sobû xatem**

His behind is bare but he has a ring on his finger.

For the sake of appearance, he sacrifices the necessities for the superfluous.

765. **ôrian yesleb fi miyet**

A naked person robbing a corpse.

A useless act, for what can one find on a corpse?

766. **orxof jenbek tetâlam elôwm**

Make yourself light, you will learn to swim.

Be flexible, not rigid, and you will adapt easily.

767. **orzoqna baxt yexdmuna bih ehl elûqul, walam torzoqna a'qal nexdmu bih ehl elbuxul**

God, give us luck so that intelligent people will serve us, and don't give us intelligence with which we will serve lucky and lazy people.

768. **oskot ula nzidek**

Keep quiet or I will hurt you more.

A bad situation can become worse; resign yourself to it, and be content.

769. **ośrob ula tayar garnek**

Drink, or break your horns.

The deer is thirsty and he finds dirty water. His choice: to drink it, or to hit his head against the rock and break his horns.

There is no choice. If you need something, you pay what they ask you for any quality, or do without.

770. **osrof torzoq**

If you spend more, you will earn more.

771. **oxtob âla wednek muś âla âynek**

Ask a girl for marriage after what you hear and not after what you see.

Honor and reputation of character are more important than beauty.

772. **ôz nefsek tsibha**

Respect your person, you will find it back.

Do not depreciate yourself; other people will respect you, and you will safeguard your dignity.

773. **qabqab elbelarej fi blèd elhiwan**

The little crow wore shoes in the land of the animals.

He is insignificant but he thinks himself very important.

774. **qa'da feddar ula zwaj elâr**

Staying home is better than a marriage of shame.

775. **qaddi elôdjèn yerja'lek modabar**

Ask a lazy person to perform a chore, he becomes an adviser.

In order to free himself from his duties, the lazy person finds excuses and pretends that he is doing that for your sake. (Example: if you tell him to cut a few branches, he will advise you that it might hurt the tree.)

776. **qad ma uledt utbaza' demmi waqt elḡasra h̲ad ma qal omi**

I gave birth many times and my blood was spilled, but in time of stress, no one said "Mother!"

Don't count on your children when you reach old age.

777. **qalb elh̲nin h̲zin**

A compassionate heart is always depressed.

Maybe because he is disappointed by the ingratitude of those he has helped.

778. **qalb safi umizan wafi**

A pure heart and a surplus weight [he gives more merchandise for your money].

He is good-natured and generous.

779. **qalu âlaś buk mèt beśśar qalu ma lqaś uxala**

They asked why his father died of starvation; he said he did not have [money] and decided not to spend it.

You can do nothing against poverty but suffer deprivation.

780. **qalu elleft idawi elêyneyn qalu a'tini enno'ma xana'ma**

They told him: "turnip will cure your eyes." He answered: "give me bread and let me become blind."

Sometimes, one prefers what is enjoyable and pleasant rather than what is useful.

781. **qalu lelqatusa âlaś uladek lwèn qalet men h̲ośmet lujuh**

They asked the female cat why her kittens were of different colors; she said because she is embarrassed to say no.

Better be embarrassed for a short time than commit the act and suffer the dire consequences.

782. **qalu onqobli áyni qalu yedi tuja'ni**

He asked him to gouge his eye; he responded that he had a pain in his hand.

He never helps anyone, always finding excuses.

783. **qalu śkun buk ya bḡal qalu xali leẖsan**

They asked the mule who his father was, he said my uncle is the horse.

The mule is a hybrid; his father is the donkey and his mother is the mare. Since he is ashamed of his father, he boasts of his uncle, the horse, his mother's brother. Applies to one who does not give you a straight answer but an indirect and embellished one, or to one who is ashamed of his parents.

784. **qalu ta'refši elôlm qalu nzid fih**

He was asked if he knew something, he said "much more."

Rather than giving you a straight and concise answer, he elaborates to the point of confusion.

785. **qalu xud surdi westorni, qalu ma telqaś baraẖ xir menni**

He said, "Take some money and keep my secret"; he answered, "You will not find a better town crier than I."

You hire someone to be your secretary (keeper of your secrets), and he turns out to be the worst divulger of secrets.

786. **qalu ya baba aya nwaliw śerfa, qalu ẖata imutu jiran el ẖawma**

He said to his father: "Let us become holy men." He answered: "Until all the neighbors in the street die."

Don't pretend to be what you are not. Everybody knows you and your origins.

787. **qalu ya baba ejmel beryal, qalu ijib rabi; qalu ya baba ejmel bemya, qalu jib tneyn**

He said to his father, "The camel costs one *ryal.*" He answered, "God will help." He said to his father, "The camel costs one hundred *ryal.*" He answered, "Go buy two camels."

It is not the price of the item that determines if you buy it or not; it is your ability to pay for it. The cost of living is a very relative thing: when you are poor, it is very high; when you are rich, it is very low.

788. **qalu ya baya' feś tbi' qalu kol śey h̠ader**

He asked the merchant what he was selling; he answered, "Everything is displayed before your eyes."

Nothing is hidden; don't ask unnecessary questions when you know the answer.

789. **qalu ya jmel ama xir ettalâ ula elhabta qalu yerzik fetneyn**

They asked the camel what was better, climbing a hill or descending a slope; he said may both be cursed.

Facing two alternatives, one worse than the other.

790. **qalu ya jmel śniya sanâtek? qalu qazaz; qalu dahar âla swabá yeddeyk usaqeyk**

He asked the camel what was his craft; he responded, a silk weaver. He said: "You look like it from seeing your fingers and toes."

When you catch someone lying and boasting about certain qualities and abilities while his appearance clearly denotes the contrary (the toes of the camel are not fit for the craft).

791. **qalu ya rebbi èt yedek, ma jawbuś; qalu ya rebbi xud yedi, xdaha**

They said: "Rabbi, give me your hand"; he did not respond. They said: "Rabbi, take my hand"; he stretched his arm and took it.

An anticlerical proverb stressing the fact that the clergy is always ready to take but never to give. In this story the rabbi was sinking in quicksand; he refused to give his hand in order to be rescued, but responded to the magic word "take."

792. **qalu ya rebbi serduki taẖ felbir qalu trifa; qalu ya rebbi serdukek taẖ felbir qalu ejri talû**

They said: "Rabbi, *my* rooster fell in the well." He said: "Forbidden to eat; not kosher." They said: "Rabbi, *your* rooster fell in the well." He said: "Run and take it out" [so that we can eat it].

An anticlerical proverb that accuses the clergy of bending the laws to serve their own interests.

793. **qalu za' qalu hèdi ellexer zaâ**

They said: "Za'." He said: "This is the last time."

"Za' " is what you say to a slow camel when you want him to run faster. This proverb is used when you ask someone for help many times and promise each time that the latest request is your last.

794. **qard mwellef ula ḡzal śrud**

A tamed monkey is better than a wild gazelle.

Nurture is more important than nature.

795. **qasulu yedu jat mniẖa letambur**

They cut off his hand, and it was very good for the drum.

Every cloud has a silver lining.

796. **qatus elmejnun ida toskotlu yakol âśatek, ida tadrbu yetjenlek**

The mad cat: if you let her do what she wants, she will eat your dinner; if you hit her, she will become angry.

Damned if you do, damned if you don't.

797. **qatus elqadi xra âla staẖna**

The cat of the qadi [religious leader] defecated on our roof.

When somebody boasts of being a relative or a close friend of the famous, based on a very sordid connection.

798. **qbar mbayed ula xyèl mśum**

A whitewashed grave is better than a bad shadow.

It is better for some bad people (like criminals, or those who bring shame to their families) to be dead than alive.

799. **qbèl ma teśri dar, śuf śkun ejjar**

Before you buy a house, check who is your neighbor.

800. **qbèl ma tḡis qis ula qyas ba'd elḡarq**

Before you set foot in the water, measure, and there is no measuring after drowning.

Story: a barber was shaving the king. When the razor was on the king's throat, he told the king: "Your majesty, I am madly in love with your daughter, and I request your consent to marry her." And he pressed the razor lightly. The king, fearing for his life, responded: "Certainly, I will never find a better son-in-law." But immediately after the shaving, the king ordered the barber's arrest and execution. Hence, before you set foot in water (or sharpen the razor), measure (the consequences).

Be prudent; don't act without considering the results of your actions.

801. **qdèr elbnadem lbèsu**

The honor of a man is his clothes.

If you dress neatly and nicely, people will respect you.

802. **qfiz h̲okam âla weyba rîya**

A legion of leaders for a small group of subjects.

Too much bureaucracy and red tape.

803. **qos erras tenśef la'ruq**

Cut off the head, the veins will dry out.

If you destroy the leader, the followers will disappear.

804. **qul lelkelb ya sidi h̲ata yeqta' bik elwed**

Call the dog master until he helps you cross the river.

When you need someone, you must respect him even if he does not deserve it.

805. **qul ma tẖab esma' ma tekrah**

Say what you like, hear what you hate.

By hearing criticism about yourself, you will mend your ways.

806. **rabi aqwa mennek ya bẖar**

God is stronger than you, ocean.

For strong, there is stronger. Everyone has his master.

807. **rabi âtani elxeyr waâtani weyn nẖotu**

God gave me wealth and also where to put it.

I have my possessions and a beautiful house to store them in. I am very happy, lacking nothing.

808. **rabi iẖab eśśokra welbnadem iẖab elfoxra**

God wants to be worshipped, and man wants to be praised.

Everyone deserves credit for his good actions or behavior; it is not a sin to be proud of one's accomplishments.

809. **rabi ya'ref èś felbeytenjala, ẖśa fi zokha ûd**

God knows what is in the eggplant; [therefore] he put a stick in its behind.

I knew what you were capable of doing (bad); therefore I took some preventive action to protect myself.

810. **rabi ya'ti elbard âla qad leḡta**

God gives the cold to fit the cover.

For those who have no blankets to cover themselves, God gives a warm temperature. One cannot lose on all counts, there is always something good to compensate.

811. **rabi ya'tina deyf nîsu fitrah**

God give us a guest, we will profit from his company.

A child is happy to have guests because the quality of food served is much better than usual.

812. **rajel blè mèl maqhur feddenya ma yeswaśi**

A man without wealth is despised; he is worth nothing in this world.

813. **raqa'ha telêt mbawta**

He patched it, but the patch shows.

You try to remedy a situation (like explaining a bad word against someone), and you make it worse.

814. **ras elfartas qrib el rabi**

The head of the bald is close to God.

The poor are always the first to be hit and hurt.

815. **ras elqartala moxmaj eś ikun qa'ha**

If the top of the basket [of fruits] is rotten, what can one expect from the bottom?

If the leaders are corrupt, certainly the people at the bottom are worse.

816. **ras mâ ejmaâ gerba'**

One head with the whole group cut off.

When one's head is cut off with so many others, it is more bearable.

Misery loves company.

817. **rasu felxra wihadan**

His head is in the excrement and he crows [like a rooster].

When you are in hot water (having legal, financial, or honor problems), you can't teach people how to behave, or boast about your actions and behavior.

818. **rdayet allah urdayet elwaldeyn**

Respect and obey God and your parents.

819. **rdayna belhem welhem ma rda bina**

We accepted the misfortune but the misfortune did not accept us.

We gave in all the way, we were ready to compromise, but still no solution.

820. **rebbi elleyl; elmra teḡleb esshor**

The rabbi [teacher] of the night; women are stronger than sorcery.

Women wield much influence over their husbands at night at the time of intimacy; they work better than sorcery.

821. **rekbuh âl bhim med yedu lezzenbil**

They allowed him to sit on the donkey, he put his hand in the sack.

You do a favor for somebody, he abuses it; he takes advantage of your kindness.

822. **rèkbu weẖdih, uẖadtu ula yenôslek**

Mount him on the horse, cushion his flanks, and keep talking to him so that he won't fall asleep.

He is asking (or expecting) too much from me, like giving him money, food, and shelter, and even entertaining his friends. He has a lot of nerve.

823. **rezq elbtati yati**

Money for the barrels [of wine] will come.

Drinkers believe that God will always send them money to buy wine; or, alcoholics spend their money on wine before anything else.

824. **rezq elxu ând elxu**

The wealth of my brother is like mine.

I am happy when my brother is wealthy.

825. **rezqi fettaqa wana mośtaqa**

My wealth is in the closet, and I am in need.

Rich but living poor, because one is afraid to use up all one's wealth and become poor. Don't be like that!

826. **riẖet omi âlik ya xalti**

The smell of my mother is on you, my aunt.

My aunt reminds me of my mother (they are sisters and look alike), and I love her all the same.

827. **rod ltami âla fomi uxellini welli jraẖni huwa idèwini**

Put my muzzle back on my mouth and leave me alone, and he who wounded me will heal me.

There are insults and injuries for which silence is best; and only the care of the person responsible could repair the damage.

828. **rqad enhar śmata lelleyl**

Sleep in the day is enemy to the night.

Because you can't sleep at night.

829. **rxos leẖrir ẖata meshu bih etnajer!**

Has silk become so cheap that they are using it to wipe pots!

How dare you behave toward me with disrespect, I who am a very honorable man! I want respect, and will not tolerate such behavior. Or: he fell from top to bottom, lost everything, including the respect of his peers.

830. **sabaq leẖsira qbel ejjama'**

He prepared the floor mat before the mosque.

Don't put the cart before the horse; everything in its own time.

831. **sabri âla ruẖi ula sbar ennas âliya**

I have to console myself [for a loss]; nobody else can console me.

832. **ṡa'dek ya latraś**

Lucky are the deaf.

Because they will not hear bad language, bad music, stories of calamities, murder, rape, etc.

833. **śah̲am elôjla tejri**

Grease the wheel, it will run.

Give a bribe, you will get things done.

834. **sah̲eb sanâtek âduk walu ikun buk ula xuk**

People of the same profession are enemies, even if they are fathers or brothers.

835. **sah̲ti xir men mèli, ida ufat sah̲ti eś bqali**

My health is better than my wealth; if I lose my health, what is left?

836. **sakar tsib ma th̲ol**

Shut [the door], you will find what to open.

If you don't shut your doors, when you return, nothing will be left to open; everything will be stolen.

837. **sam śna ubat àla djaja mentna**

He fasted for one year and dined with a rotten chicken.

He waited for so long for something, and when he finally got it (or did it), it was rotten, crooked, or wrong.

838. **saqaflu yeśtah̲lek**

Clap your hands for him, he will dance for you.

He is very impressionable; he will dance to your tune.

839. **saq fessarwal welmo'som felkom, ma iqabel essoltan kèn elmebsem welfom**

A leg in the trousers and a sleeve on the arm, [but] the only thing that faces the king is the smile and the face.

Whatever clothes you wear and however beautiful you are, you will be judged by your expression and by what you say.

840. **śaqi ula moh̲taj**

Tired is better than needy.

Work hard and help yourself so that you will never need the help of others.

841. **saq lebhim tji zokra?**

Can the leg of a donkey become a flute?

A son of a tramp (or beggar, or drunkard, etc.) can never become a respectable person and be successful.

842. **saqu marbuta beh̲bel ijib elkusksi welh̲am**

His leg is tied with a rope, he brings grain and meat.

Whatever a man's occupation, he must provide for his family.

843. **saraq men ànd elàser**

He is a thief from the morning hours.

He can't wait to steal, he starts early in the morning. He is a big thief.

844. **saraq ufiyedu śamâ**

A thief, and a candle in his hand.

Somebody who has the audacity, the nerve, to steal and not hide his act.

845. **sarj h̲san àla dhar bhim**

Harness of a horse on the back of a donkey.

A well-dressed person who is dumb.

846. **śart elâzeb âl hajala welli sbiya naxdok**

The bachelor's condition to the widow: become a virgin, I will marry you.

His conditions are impossible. We can never make a deal with him: he is not serious about reaching an agreement.

847. **sasi umetśarat ubab daru âli**

A beggar, very choosy, and his door high.

Beggars can't be choosers; if you are in need, accept what is given to you and be thankful for it.

848. **sbah̲ elxeyr ya jari enti fi darek wana fi dari**

Good morning, neighbor! You are in your house and I am in mine.

In order to preserve our good relationship, it is better to keep some distance between us. Familiarity breeds contempt.

849. **śed mśumek ula ijik ma aśwam**

Hold on to the bad lest you should get worse.

If you have something not entirely satisfactory (job, husband, etc.), it is better to resign yourself to your fate than to try to change it, because you may fall into a worse situation.

850. **śefti thèrèt ubenti ma trabèt**

My lip is burning and my daughter is not yet educated.

It is very difficult to raise children; talking does not help much.

851. **semnet udâfet welôrs ma raha**

She became fat, then she became skinny, and the wedding didn't see her.

She has done everything she can to attract a husband, but to no avail. One does a lot to please another, but the other does not respond in kind.

852. **sès ermel ma tâlih, yekber witih sèsha; farx ezna ma trabih, yekber uyerja' lnèsha**

Don't erect a high building on sand foundations; it will crumble after some time. Don't raise an illegitimate child; he will grow up and become like his natural progenitors.

853. **seyeb esshih uśed errih**

He abandoned the strong and solid and held onto the wind.

Never throw away what is certain for what is in doubt.

854. **sfenja utahet felâsal**

A spongy bun, and it fell in honey.

A greedy person who found money! Somebody waiting for an opportunity and it comes to him.

855. **śkun elmahbul elli yezrá fuq esstah ula elli iśèrku**

Who is the crazy one, the one who sows seeds on the roof, or the one who agrees to be his partner?

Taking part in an action makes you an accomplice, and therefore responsible. Or: this is stupid, and this is even more stupid.

856. **śkun fayeq bik ya sareq ezzeyt**

Who is aware of you, oil thief.

Do your own thing, don't worry about what they say.

857. **śkun fxar la'rusa omha ula xaletha**

Who praised the bride? Her mother or her aunt?

Praise coming from close relatives is not credible because they are supposed to do that.

858. **śkun iqul baba xaray kèn dabar usaheb ray**

No one will say "My father is incontinent." Everyone will say "He is a man of advice and wisdom."

Never speak ill of members of your family because it will turn against you.

859. **śkun iqul lessayd fomok abxar**

Who will tell the lion that he has bad breath?

Nobody dares to insult the powerful.

860. **śkun iśemmet fik âdak kèn rajlek ula dnak**

Whose action makes your enemies happy [when you are in distress]? Your husband's or your children's.

861. **śkun izur elḡorba kèn elqatus ula elkelba**

Who pays a visit to the exiled? Only the cat or the dog.

The people who are exiled from their country are always lonely.

862. **śkun jè melqbar ujèb lexbar**

Who came back from the grave and told the story?

Nobody knows what happens after death.

863. **śkun mśè lelqbar ujèb lexbar**

Who went to the grave and brought the information?

Nobody knows what happens after death. Or: this affair is very mysterious.

864. **śkun ya'ref elqoba xeyt ula stoba**

Who knows the bottom of the pool, if it is good thread or junk?

You can never know what is hidden and not apparent.

865. **smala âl mabar ida yetḡabar**

God protect the velvet from being covered with dust!

Ironic: you think yourself holy, untouchable; we can't even approach you for fear of contaminating you; we can't even talk to you for fear of hurting you. Who do you think you are?

866. **sob elma fi zok ettor**

Pour water in the bull's ass.

This is usually done after the bull is slaughtered for the purpose of skinning and cleaning him. But it is of no help. A useless act.

867. **śrab elxel ula btaltu**

Drinking vinegar or nothing at all.

Two contradictory explanations: 1. It is better to drink sour wine than no wine at all; i.e., accept whatever you can find even if it is not perfect. 2. If you can find only sour wine, don't drink at all; i.e., go first class or stay home.

868. **śuf beytu woxtob bentu**

See his house and ask for the hand of his daughter.

Before you get married, you had better check her family and their house, because she will keep your house the same way.

869. **śuf elwej qasat felẖam**

Look at the face, and cut the meat sparingly.

By looking at the face of a person, you will know if he is healthy or sick, and you distribute your food accordingly.

You can't hide your feelings; your face is like a mirror.

870. **śuf xuha fezqaq uzidha fesdaq**

See her brother in the street, and raise her dowry.

Family members are alike and each one is responsible for the others.

871. **swaba' yeddeyk muś qad qad**

Your fingers are not the same.

Even brothers don't look alike.

872. **taba' elbum yeddik lelxla**

Follow the owl, he will take you to the desert.

If you associate with bad people, they will ruin you.

873. **taba' essareq ẖata lbab eddar**

Follow the thief to the threshold.

Don't accuse anyone of evil intentions; judge other people only by their actions.

874. **tafi leftila ennsa elkol fard nila**

Put out the light, all women are alike.

875. **taẖt jnaẖ eddebana ula ejjabana**

Under the wings of the fly is better than in the cemetery.

The worst kind of life is better than death. Better to suffer than to die.

876. **tâjeb el maslux felmadbuẖ**

The one who is lacerated all over is surprised to see the one whose throat has been cut.

Don't reproach others for having the same faults as yours.

877. **tâlmu leẖjama fi rus litama**

They learned to cut hair on the heads of the orphans.

Barbers' apprentices practice their skill on the heads of orphans because they can't pay. Don't use me as a guinea pig for your experiments.

878. **tama nas huma huma, tama nas metl la'sal felgerjuma, tama nas melkelmot ula huma**

There are people who are not good and not bad; there are people like honey in your throat; and there are people who are worse than the angel of death.

You have good and bad in everything.

879. **târek erriẖ mâ lebẖar ja ettaksir felmrèkeb**

The wind had a fight with the sea, and the boats got broken.

Innocent victims always pay for the conflicts between others more powerful than they.

880. **taret essekra uẖadret lemdeynia**

You are sober again, and the creditors are here.

Alcohol can make you forget your problems only temporarily; you must wake up to reality.

881. **târku lexwat ijed âl mehbulat**

The sisters had a fight, and the fools believed it.

When sisters (or brothers) quarrel, it does not last; they will soon reconcile.

882. **tawel ônqok ya ḡarnuq**

Stretch your neck, crane.

Like the bird who stretches his neck as an act of pride, a braggart deserves this comment.

883. **tbib esqoli qatlu sanû**

Doctor Skoli was killed by his assistant.

Story: when Doctor Skoli, a surgeon, was unable to extract a frog from the belly of a patient, his assistant gave him advice—to burn the feet of the frog that were gripping the organs. Doctor Skoli followed his assistant's advice and the frog let go one leg after the other. Doctor Skoli died of shame.

This applies to someone who is directed by his children or his subordinates, and is humiliated.

884. **tebdil essruj raẖa**

Changing the harnesses gives some comfort.

Changing houses, jobs, activities, is relaxing.

885. **tekber ya kenna wetśuf ma śeft ana**

You, daughter-in-law, will get older and see what I have seen.

Your daughter-in-law will hate you as you hate me. The world turns and we pay for everything.

886. **tendem ma ndem essayad âla kelbu**

You will regret, the same way the hunter regretted his dog.

Story: a hunter had a dog so faithful that he let him baby-sit his infant. One day, he came back and found his son bleeding all over and crying, and the dog beside him. Instinctively, the hunter pulled out his gun and shot the dog. Then he pushed the dog aside and found a dead snake under him. He understood that the dog had fought courageously to protect the baby from the snake, and had killed the snake. The hunter bitterly regretted his action.

Don't act thoughtlessly in a fit of passion.

887. **tesma' xbar eddar ând essḡar**

You hear the house secrets from the little ones.

Children cannot hide anything; they will tell you everything about their house and their family. Don't tell them any secrets.

888. **t̲h̲ab elh̲aq ula h̲waśih?**

Do you want truth and justice or their fringes?

You say this to somebody who persistently refuses to hear the truth.

889. **tneyn yeḡlbu walu ikunu yelâbu**

Two will win, even playing.

There is strength in numbers.

890. **ubaya utalh̲iqa**

A plague and another plague.

From bad to worse.

891. **ûda wah̲da ma ttala' duxan**

One single branch does not produce smoke.

And certainly no fire. Strength is in numbers.

892. **ufa belâdala**

He is finished with notaries.

He has lost everything, and the notary public has testified to his real bankruptcy.

893. **ulad elâm yeẖmiw eddem**

Cousins make the blood boil.

When your cousins are attacked, you come to their defense because they are family.

894. **ulad Sidi Bedda waẖed ibi' uwaẖed iqul roda**

The sons of Sidi Bedda, one sells and one cancels the sale.

There are many chiefs, which creates confusion. One person only should be in command.

895. **ulèthem qẖab a'qabhem dgagez**

They start as prostitutes, they end up as fortune-tellers.

When someone is no longer good for a job, he does what he can to survive.

896. **ultu tfaq wa'qabu slama**

Reaching an agreement in the beginning means peace in the end.

When you make a deal, be sure to work out all the details very clearly for both parties; that way, you will not quarrel later about the terms because of misunderstandings.

897. **usax ezzeyt ula rebẖ etmar**

The dirt from oil is better than the gain from dates.

It is better to sell oil than dates because customers like to taste the dates, which will cause a loss.

898. **waẖdi fessrir wala rajel dalil**

Alone in bed is better than with a worthless man.

No company is better than bad company.

899. **waẖed âtah waẖed lwah, wahed darbu darba kasarlu nxah̄**

He has given to one, he has twisted the second, and he has broken the bones of the third.

Life is a matter of luck; who knows what lies in store for us.

900. **waẖed belloqma lfomu laxor belxeśba lêynu**

For one, a good mouthful of food; for the other, a stick in the eye.

Some are luckier than others; or, there is a double standard.

901. **waẖed belôsma ulaxor bejerian ejjuf**

One is constipated, the other has diarrhea.

He exaggerates in this direction, and you exaggerate in the other. One must always look for the happy medium.

902. **waẖed iqul hay yemlaha, waẖed iqul hay yufaha**

One says "Hi" and it will fill, one says "Hi" and it will empty.

There are people who are lucky—anything they touch turns to gold—and there are the opposites.

903. **waẖed ma inaẖiś xeśmu men wejju**

One does not cut one's nose from his face.

One can't cut himself off from his family.

904. **waẖed msarnu mbazâ ulaxor qalu a'tini trayef lelqatusa**

One's intestines are spilled over, and the other says "give me some for my cat."

While all are fighting a serious situation, he comes and

worries only about trivial matters. He is very callous and insensitive.

905. **wah̲ed qalbu âla tamra, wah̲ed qalbu âla jamra**

One's heart is on a date [fruit], and the other's heart is on fire.

While some people are happy, some are hurting and suffering. That's destiny, God's will.

906. **wah̲ed yakol eddarb uwah̲ed iôdlu**

One gets the beating, and the other counts it for him.

Only those who suffer feel the pain, not those who just keep records.

907. **wah̲ed yaxod leltu, wah̲ed yaxod ôltu, wah̲ed yaxod darba âla kelwtu**

One marries a lady, one marries a burden, and one marries a blow on his kidney.

Marriage is a matter of luck.

908. **wah̲let elmenjel felqolla**

Caught like a sickle in the jar.

You can't take it out without breaking it or breaking the jar. No solution to the conflict; both sides will lose.

909. **wakaltek leknawejlu, ŝarabtek ma lagdah̲, welli ixalet tonj ḡeyr men tonju yestahel taksir ejjnah̲**

I fed you fine grain, I gave you pure water to drink, but he who associates with other than his own kind deserves the breaking of his wings.

Story: an owl was starving, desperate for grain and water. He met a sparrow who volunteered to help and to show the owl a nice place, but it was far away and the sparrow suggested that the owl take him on his back and fly him there. And so it was, but after the owl ate and drank, he took the sparrow on his back for the return flight and then dropped him; the fall broke the sparrow's wing.

This is a model of ingratitude, returning evil for good. Also, a lesson: don't associate with people you don't know.

910. **waqt elmeśmèś tlata yam wèś.**

The time of the apricots, three days and something.

This is of very short duration, ephemeral.

911. **waqt elwasâ s̲habi sebâ, waqt elḡasra âmlu fesâ**

When I was well-off, I had seven friends; when I became poor, they all fled.

912. **waqt essyada mśa elkelb yetqada**

At the time of the hunting, the dog went to relieve himself.

Just when you need someone (or something), he (it) is not available.

913. **waqtli h̲ajti bik ya weji xarbśuk leqtates**

When I needed you, my face, the cats scratched you.

Accidents always happen at the most inopportune times. When one needs something very badly, it doesn't work.

914. **waqtli kont enti tzamar kont ana ntamar**

While you were playing and singing, I was working.

If you are poor now and I am rich, it is because you have been lazy.

One should prepare oneself well for life.

915. **waqtli kuna jazzara ma jawnèś la'laleś**

When we were butchers, we could not find sheep.

When a person is young and can still enjoy life and women, he does not have the opportunity.

916. **waqt ma this wetbis h̲ot elqarmis**

When you are destitute and desperate, set your [cobbler's] table.

A craft, manual labor, will not make you rich, but will save you from hunger and despair.

917. **warini sehmi felqasà ukulu**

Show me my share in the plate, and eat it.

I am mainly interested in justice and respect, not in the actual thing or material reward.

918. **weldek ida iwelli sabatek qad sabatu obôd men xlatu**

When your son's shoe becomes as big as yours, stop associating with him.

Give independence to your grown-up children; let them fend for themselves; don't interfere in their private lives.

919. **weld elfar yetla' h̲afar**

The son of the mouse will be a good digger.

Like father, like son. Aptitudes and skills are inherited and/or nurtured.

920. **werta ula h̲arta ula darba beqlem**

An inheritance, or a plowed land, or a trick with a pen.

These are three ways to become rich: inherit, work, or steal (embezzle funds by forging documents).

921. **weyn babek ya suwa**

Where is your door, wide country!

We can't find a small thing in a big thing (a needle in a haystack); or, we cannot extricate ourselves from a bad situation.

922. **weyn flusek ya h̲amar fessfih̲a welmosmar**

Where has your money gone, donkey rider? Into horseshoes and nails.

Sometimes, the expenses to produce income (a donkey rider transports people and merchandise to make a living) eat up most of the income.

923. **weyn fluskom ya ihud fessbut wela'yud**

Where has your money gone, Jews? Into the sabbaths and holidays.

924. **weyn nẖotok ya tbaq elward**

Where shall I put you, tray of roses?

When a person is welcomed, well treated, and respected; everybody would like to have him as a guest.

925. **xabi ma takol umatxabiś ma teqdi**

You may postpone eating, but you may not postpone doing housework.

926. **xaf men rabi uxaf melli ma ixafś men rabi**

Fear God and fear those who do not fear God.

927. **xalas śa'rek yesḡar, xamal darek tekber**

Comb your hair, it will be smaller; clean up your house, it will be bigger.

Order and neatness improve appearances greatly.

928. **xayt edhab iroq uma yetqata'ś**

The gold thread may weaken but will not break.

A person of quality will not become a crook under stress.

929. **xedmet elleyl śmata lenhar**

Night work is a revenge on the day.

Because one must sleep during the day.

930. **xedmet ennhar ma fiha âr**

A job done in daylight cannot carry shame with it.

Anything which you do in broad daylight, rather than secretly, is honorable.

931. **xeffet leqdèm txallaf endèm**

Lightness of heel will leave regret.

If you do things too quickly, you will regret.

932. **xella miytu memdud umśa yendeb âla Âbud**

He left his kin's corpse lying and went to mourn Âbud.

He takes care of other people's problems but forgets his own.

933. **xelli la'duk uma testh̲aqś leh̲bibek**

Leave an inheritance to your enemy and don't rely on your friend's help.

Save money, even if it means leaving it, after your death, to people you don't like. This is better than spending everything and, if in need, asking for help from friends.

934. **xobzti uxobztek welbuqal beynatna**

Your bread and my bread, and the water pitcher between us.

Let's keep our assets separated; let's not share anything; each one his own. That way, we will avoid problems, and continue to respect each other.

935. **xobz uma wahna ula xobz ulh̲am uham**

Bread and water in peace is better than bread and meat in trouble.

Happiness is not found in material possessions but in peace of mind and harmony.

936. **xoltot sareq men śrutat elh̲abs uxoltot âlem men slah̲ eddin**

The friends of a thief come from prisons, and those of the educated person come from law-abiding people.

Birds of a feather flock together.

937. **xrejt menek ya kerś omi inśala tjib âfrit**

I left you, my mother's belly, now you may give birth to a demon.

I am safe, after me the deluge! An act of cruel selfishness.

938. **xud bent lasul idur âliha ezman ma th̲ul**

Take a wife from a good family; even if she becomes poor, she will not stray from her good habits.

939. **xud elbentek h̲awki h̲ata tujedla rajel**

Marry your daughter to a wool weaver until you find a better husband.

Wool weaving is considered a low-status trade, compared to silk weaving.

940. **xud elôlm men rus elfkaren!**

Take knowledge [of science] from the heads of the tortoises.

Don't listen to ignorant people, you never learn; or, what does he know about this? What are his credentials?

941. **xud elweldek weyn yetma' ulbentek weyn teśba'**

Marry your son where he can profit, and your daughter where she can eat her fill.

942. **xudha men yed eśśebân ida ja' uma taxodhaś men yed ejjuân ida śba'**

Take a gift from the hand of the satiated person who became hungry, and not from the hungry person who became satiated.

943. **xud leklam elli ibekik, ma taxodś leklam elli idah̲kek**

Accept the words that make you cry, and not the words that make you laugh.

944. **xud men taynek yemlas, ida ma iji borma iji keskas**

Take from your own clay, it will be smooth; if it can't become a pot, it will become a pan.

Marry within your own group, clan, or family, and you will have no problems; if it is not perfect, at least it is good.

945. **xud sèhmek filuel walu fi darb elkef**

Take your share among the first even if it is a slap in the face.

Don't delay receiving what is due to you because you might lose it.

946. **xuyè men baba kif erriẖ feššababa, xuyè men omi kif la'sal fifomi**

My half-brother from my father's side is like the wind in a flute; my half-brother from my mother's side is like honey in my mouth.

This proverb stresses the importance of motherhood.

947. **ya dèxel beyn edfar welẖam ya xarej bentuna**

What comes between the fingernail and the flesh will come out stinking.

Don't get involved in a domestic fight, between husband and wife, or brothers; you will be the loser.

948. **ya dèxel elmasr mènèk aluf**

You who enter Egypt, there are thousands like you.

You are not original, what you do is not special, don't think you are the only one.

949. **ya ẖafer ẖofrot essew ya tayaẖ fiha**

He who digs a hole for the other will fall into it.

The evil you do, or plan to do, to others, will return against you.

950. **ya hajajel qumu berjal**

You, widows, give the men free room and board.

The lowest and weakest people, in a group or society, carry the heavy burden of providing for the strong, the able, and the wealthy.

951. **ya ẖbaq mènèk sbaq**

You, good-smelling plant, there have been [others] like you before.

Said to someone bragging about his accomplishments: "You are not the first to do that."

952. **yajura felh̲ayt wala yaquta felxayt**

A brick in the wall is better than a pearl on a string.

Value and respect for real estate.

953. **yakol elḡala wiseb elmella**

He eats the fruit and insults the person.

He bites the hand that feeds him; he is ungrateful.

954. **yakol etto'm uyexra âssonar**

He eats the bait [food] and defecates on the hook.

Ingratitude.

955. **yakol wigor kif leh̲mama**

He eats and grumbles like the pigeon.

He is never happy whatever you give him; he always complains.

956. **yakol xobztu uyetma' ferbaya' mta' sah̲bu**

He eats his loaf of bread and takes advantage of his friend by eating a quarter of his.

Greed and dishonesty.

957. **ya lèhi behmum ennas wahmumek ya mśum kdas**

You are taking care of other people's problems, and your problems are piling up.

Mind your own business; or, you spend your time helping others at the expense of your own family.

958. **ya men raśi ònba fi wed ezzbib**

Who can see a grape in a river of raisins?

It is very difficult to find something lost in a huge area; a needle in a haystack.

959. **ya meskin mennek ktir**

O, poor man, there are so many like you.

As a way of consolation, you say to someone in distress: "You are not alone." Misery loves company.

960. **ya mrabi ulad ennas yelli tsob elma felkeskas**

Raising other people's children is like pouring water into the colander [full of holes].

A proverb against adoption.

961. **ya nhar elli tmut omok meymuna iqum essyah fi rades**

The day Mother Mimuna dies, there will be an uproar in Rades.

Story: a new midwife settled in the city of Rades. Many years passed by; she grew old and was venerated by everyone for her dedication and kindness. When her neighbors and friends inquired about her health, she responded: "The day Mother Mimuna dies, there will be an uproar in Rades." This was an enigma until she died: when the women came to wash her body before the burial, they found . . . that she had been a man . . . for forty-five years. Hence, the uproar.

You think everything is fine now, wait until you see the day of reckoning.

962. **ya qatel erruh weyn mèś truh**

You, murderer, you have nowhere to go.

Justice, or vengeance, will catch up to you. You can never commit a crime and get away with it. You will pay for it here.

963. **ya'ref rabi uyexra felqamh**

He knows God and he defecates on the wheat.

He knows the rules of law and religion, but does not observe them. A hypocrite.

964. **yarmi ennar âtben wiqul eddoxan mneyn**

He throws the fire on the straw and asks where the smoke comes from.

He causes the trouble and pretends he is an innocent trying to help. A hyprocrite.

965. **ya ŝèri elhem betqiq**

You are buying trouble with flour [money].

This is not some kind of trouble that came from God and you could do nothing about. This is trouble you provoked, you asked for, you even paid for.

966. **ya ŝèri elh̲ut fi bah̲ru**

You are buying the fish that is still in the ocean.

You buy a pig in a poke. You buy something without seeing it, or make a deal without checking.

967. **ya ŝèri qatus fi ŝkara**

You are buying a cat in a sack!

Don't buy a pig in a poke. Caveat emptor! *Always check thoroughly before buying anything.*

968. **ya tbib elômyan dèwi âynek elâwra**

You, doctor of the blind, cure your own blind eye.

Take care of your own problems before you get involved in other people's problems. Mind your own business.

969. **ya xsaret elful lelli ma ânduŝ zrus**

It is a pity to waste fava beans on someone who has no teeth.

This is said about someone who cannot (or does not) enjoy what he has, like a stingy rich person, or a cowardly strong person.

970. **yebla' essèkina bdamha**

He swallows the knife with its blood.

He cleans up all traces; he does not leave any proof of his crime behind him.

971. **yebra ejjorh̲ utebra àlih edmida ukelmet essew ma tebraś tbèt utesbah̲ jdida**

The wound will heal, but a bad word will not; it will renew itself every morning.

It is easier to forget and forgive a physical injury than a verbal offense.

972. **yed farḡa uloxra mafiha śey**

One of his hands is empty, and the other has nothing in it.

He is completely destitute; or, he has no looks and no brains.

973. **yedi uyed elqabla yetla' litim a'war**

My hand with the hand of the midwife, the baby will come out one-eyed.

Too many cooks spoil the broth.

974. **yedu felqasâ uâynu fi mulat eddar**

His hand is in the plate, and his eye is on the hostess.

Someone who pretends to do something but his interest is elsewhere; he has ulterior motives.

975. **yedu fi ònqu welbarah̲ urah**

His hand in his throat and the town crier behind him.

He lost everything, his possessions and his reputation. Total despair.

976. **yed wah̲da ma tsafaqś**

One hand cannot applaud.

Union makes strength.

977. **yelâb âla śeffet elbuqal**

He plays on the edges of the jar.

He is very able and shrewd.

978. **yelâb mâ eśśitan itayar mennu ka'ba**

He plays with the devil and wins one from him.

He is very smart, very astute; he not only saves himself from bad situations but comes out the winner.

979. **yemśi lemli<u>h</u> fi jorot leqbi<u>h</u>**

The good is lost after the bad.

Good people pay for the mistakes of bad people.

980. **yemśi musa fi trab farûn**

Moses will go in the dust of the Pharaoh.

The good will be destroyed by evil; the innocent will pay for the crimes of others.

981. **yenâl din kès eddheb elli nobzoq fih eddem**

Cursed be the golden glass in which I spit blood.

What good does wealth do for you if you have no health to enjoy it?

982. **yendeb âla martbuh fedlam**

He mourns his stepmother in the dark.

He pretends to cry at the death of his (hated) stepmother, and since nobody sees him, he claims that he does it in the dark. A hyprocrite.

983. **yenki ru<u>h</u>u yeḡsi badayh**

He loses his mind and castrates himself [thinking he is hurting others].

Your evil thoughts, or acts, will hurt you primarily.

984. **yenśed âl besbasa umen zra'ha umen kèn fiha wasta**

He asks about the fennel, who planted it, and who was the agent.

He asks too much; he is a nerd.

985. **yeslah̲ rayek ma slah̲ ray elh̲alwani, yeśri belqontar wibi' belmosmar**

May God improve your mind as he did for the candymaker who buys by the ton and sells by the ounce.

Patience is virtue.

986. **yesraq elmanbar wiba'bes elimam**

He steals the podium and gives the finger to the priest.

He is very shrewd; he will always get what he wants.

987. **yestah̲fad ànoxala wibaza' essmid**

He is very careful about the bran but wasteful with the flour.

Penny wise and pound foolish.

988. **yetâlmu fi xat elimama wensaw xathom**

They have been learning the ways of the dove, and they forgot their own ways.

Stick to your own customs and culture; don't imitate strangers.

989. **yetbeddel wadû uma yetbeddelś tabû**

His destiny will change but his character will not.

One is unable to change one's own character.

990. **yexdem âla uladu ama ulad uladu yezi**

He works for his children and that is enough; he does not have to work for his grandchildren.

Each one must shoulder his own responsibilities, no more.

991. **yexdem jhennem wimut belbard**

He works in hell and dies of cold.

No retribution for hard work; ingratitude.

992. **yodxol men âyn elyebra wiqul mawsêk ya melk allah**

He enters the eye of the needle, and he says how wide God created you.

He is very handy, or lucky, and can get by easily; he can do, and succeed in, everything.

993. **yoh̲sob nefsu kebda uhuwa basla mah̲ruqa**

He thinks himself to be liver, but he is no more than burned onion.

This is said of people who are infatuated with themselves and are worth nothing.

994. **yoktru la'muma fellayam lemśuma**

The number of uncles grows in bad times.

In bad times, when poverty and hunger are prevalent, people will remember that they have an uncle somewhere who could help them with food, or a loan; hence, the increase in the number of uncles.

995. **yoqh̲bu** uyaxdu ettrek

They whore and they marry the Turks.

During Turkish rule, when the Turks were at the highest level of the social ladder, it was a big success for a girl to marry one.

Applies to a situation where one is not good but succeeds in life.

996. **yoqtol leh̲neś btermtu**

He kills the snake with his behind.

He is so secretive that even when he is attacked by a snake and his life is in danger, he tries to kill the snake with his behind, sitting down on it (which is impossible), rather than call for help and reveal his "secret."

997. **yufa elberśem welh̲rir utofdol elmśuma fessrir**

Satin and silk will disappear, and what will be left is the ugly woman in bed.

A proverb for somebody who marries an ugly or handicapped woman for her wealth.

998. **yufa mèl ejjeddeyn utoqôd sanêt elyeddeyn**

The wealth of the fathers will disappear and only handicraft will remain.

One must rely on one's personal skills and not on inheritance.

999. **zid âla âyśa mendil uxayśa**

Put on Âyśa [already ugly] a napkin and a rag.

Making an already bad situation even worse.

1000. **zir mtekki la idah̲ak ula ibekki**

A jug leaning against the wall neither makes you laugh nor makes you cry.

This person is like a jug; he does not understand anything; he does not feel anything; he is not a human being.

1001. **zman elma'kus ednabi iwelliw rus**

In crazy times, the tails become heads.

It is a bad sign when the ignorant command the intelligent, when parents fear their children, when teachers are powerless in their classrooms . . .

Thematic Index

bad company: [proverb number(s)] 39, 125, 217, 450, 697, 704, 872, 936
death: 333, 334, 335, 798
destiny: 79, 92, 263
education: 529, 695, 714
friendship: 420, 484, 591, 740, 911, 933
God: 82, 407, 806, 811
government: 495, 549
guests: 112, 113, 119, 120, 128, 129, 588, 623
hypocrisy: 421, 542, 982
ingratitude: 18, 26, 350, 478, 559, 821, 953, 954
intemperance: 12, 16, 19
keeping up with the Joneses: 21, 458
love: 412, 430, 470, 471, 472
luck: 422, 474, 476, 481
moderation: 522, 523, 524, 525
money: 36, 42, 77, 81, 92, 104, 135, 169, 198, 210, 211, 251, 285, 317, 318, 324, 325, 367, 444, 480, 585, 587, 812, 922, 981, 987, 998
morality: 203, 234, 303, 310, 311, 381, 503, 876, 957, 968
mother: 251, 252, 258, 339, 672, 776
nature/nurture: 60, 794
neighbors: 511, 512, 619, 673, 741, 799, 848
parents/children: 6, 93, 309, 408, 475, 647, 719, 723, 753, 761, 783, 858, 881, 903, 918, 960
partnership: 84, 453, 629, 973
patience: 293, 387
philosophical: 127, 133, 138, 143, 149, 228, 295, 296, 329, 390, 391, 392, 423, 448, 452, 463, 483, 608, 609, 732

precepts: 52, 74, 75, 97, 98, 163, 467
prudence: 44, 241, 247, 274, 279, 364, 677, 690, 691, 737, 836
relativity: 152, 155, 568
resignation: 298, 376, 399, 516
responsibility: 291, 292, 294, 307
sacrifice: 548, 550, 574, 932
self-interest: 97, 101, 300, 410, 473, 479, 487, 651, 668, 708, 756, 804, 831, 937
silence: 7, 70, 187, 278, 324, 534
social relations: 117, 118, 142, 277, 280, 283, 312
things in time: 64, 65, 66, 68, 436, 439
women: 38, 328, 336, 337, 419, 874, 997